CORPORATIONS
WITHOUT CONSCIENCE

CORPORATIONS WITHOUT CONSCIENCE

AND OUR RESPONSIBILITY AS WOULD-BE STAKEHOLDERS TO CAUSE THEM TO CHANGE

KEN WESSEL

iUniverse, Inc.
Bloomington

CORPORATIONS WITHOUT CONSCIENCE AND OUR RESPONSIBILITY AS WOULD-BE STAKEHOLDERS TO CAUSE THEM TO CHANGE

iUniverse books may be ordered through booksellers or by contacting:

iUniverse
1663 Liberty Drive
Bloomington, IN 47403
www.iuniverse.com
1-800-Authors (1-800-288-4677)

ISBN: 978-1-4620-4964-6 (sc)
ISBN: 978-1-4620-4965-3 (ebk)

Printed in the United States of America

iUniverse rev. date: 08/24/2011

DEDICATIONS

This book is dedicated to:

Sandi my wife, who supported me through long hours at work, extensive travels, cared for five active children and constantly challenged me to work for perfection.

Our children; Leslie, Marc, Tracy, Karyn, Gretchen and their spouses who are diligent in service to family, community, and employers.

My parents Sophie, Henry, siblings Genie, Norma, Paul, Susie, Nicky (who are true to core values and lived life as supportive partners) and the farming community where I grew up and instilled core values that have lasted a lifetime. And my in-laws, Eleanor and Ted Zaetsch who were a constant source of support for a growing and dynamic family.

Charlle Krone who opened my mind to higher levels of thinking about designing organizations and developing them and their individual members.

Charles Eberle who was my mentor in Procter & Gamble and guided me through a career that was challenging, interesting and a laboratory in understanding how organizations work.

Craig DeForest and Don Miller whose review, critique, encouragement and suggestions were a considerable asset in completing this book.

Our Treaty Line Ranch community; Assum, Bodtker, Clark, Decker, Duncan, Holliday, Krone, Miller, Narburgh, Press, Rabenold and Wessel whose workshops and wisdom promoted our development as individuals, married couples, families and community.

Ken Wessel

Members of Procter & Gamble, SaraLee, and client organizations who not only became friends but contributed to my understanding of relationships between organizations, their stakeholders and values and principles that enabled the world to become a better place.

Ken Wessel: March 20, 2011

CHAPTER LISTING SECTION ONE

Section one details abuse of stakeholders and neglect of fulfilling their needs; Corporations and Corporate Officials tend to take them for granted and feel free to with-hold filling their needs (however the squeaky wheel, Wall Street) is favored over other stakeholders. Corporate Officials aim to take care of themselves in terms of Compensation, Power based on Chain of Command and exercise of authority even though this exercise involves serious errors of judgment and misdirection of the business. This section unfolds in a logical way to depict issues and problems that Corporations generate.

I.   Stakeholder betrayal: Benedict Arnold would be proud
An examination of critical nature of living systems as source of value to stakeholders and tendency of many Corporate Officials to establish closed systems to regulate value delivered to stakeholders as means to retain value for self service to own desires.

II.   Stock ownership, impotence and trashing owner's assets
Points out alliance between Wall Street insiders and Corporate Officials that aims to promote self—interest at expense of actual owners/stock holders.

III.   Biting the hand that feeds us
Highlights tactics of corporations that emphasize size and power over suppliers that aim to pressure them to lowest cost and extend special treatment that weakens value chain and reduces value to customers.

IV.   Customer beware
Points out collusion between Government and Corporate Officials that not only deny Stakeholders their rights, but also due to lack of conscience ignores doing what is right, giving rise to behavior that ultimately leads to declining values, destruction of free enterprise system and loss in positive spirit of our country.

Ken Wessel

V.   Sustainability: an exercise of insufficiency
Calls attention to the fact that corporate organizations exist by accident rather than by design and self-serving emphasis on sustaining the physical environment that becomes a fool's errand if the organization itself is not sustainable.

VI.   Setting the stage for self-destruction
Exposure of inbuilt flaws that cause Corporate Officials to react unconsciously and obsessively to external threat and adversity, placing welfare of the organization and its stakeholders at risk.

VII.   Cost reduction madness: a terminal addiction
Addiction of Corporate Officials to concept that "lean and mean" is attractive to Wall Street, will increase executive control and income and will be tolerated passively by customers and other stakeholders.

VIII.   Diversity programs: exercise of irony:
Depicts self-serving, cynical and patronizing approach to diversity programs that is self-defeating of fundamental values by assigning people to classes as if their membership was homogeneous, at expense of individual uniqueness.

IX.   Empowerment hoax: seduction, coercion, delusion of control
Exposes myth that those in power wish to and are able to empower others.

X.   Job descriptions: pact with the devil
Calls attention to common practice by those in authority of writing job descriptions that impose organization control over the way work is done, impose strict boundaries, and emphasize "nose to the grindstone" approach to work.

XI.   Where have all the leaders gone?
Contrasts what effective leaders are and do with behavior of Corporate Officials that undermines and compromises potential for effective leadership.

XII. Self serving motives: Waste without remorse

Active conscience treats waste of any kind as an ultimate taboo, yet Corporate Officials freely waste time, energy, talent and resources in order to serve own desires.

Ken Wessel

CHAPTER LISTING: SECTION TWO

Section two generates a number of approaches that aim to resolve issues and problems detailed in section one. Resolution of issues and problems allow stakeholder needs to become more readily satisfied and reconciling of issues that allow Corporations to become more of a force for doing what's right and serving a greater good.

Leadership development is the key to a desirable future
The Leadership Development Forum challenges members of natural work groups to deal with significant real world subjects in real time and to develop an action orientation toward leading team based pursuit of opportunity and resolution of issues, with a sense of urgency and authority.
Consciously designed organizations
It introduces a new perspective on organization design and development that aims to generate continuing research, study, understanding and application so that we use our organizational roles to upgrade design and promote increasing rate of healthy growth.

Self-empowerment: choosing our own course in life
Presents a perspective of empowerment as a natural pursuit for all human beings as we aim for increasing authority, command and control of our everyday affairs and the course of our lives.

Will to become . . . to do . . . to be
Advances premises about faith, hope, commitment as elements of will to become more of our true self and to live life as a continuously evolving, developing person.

Change, renewal and regeneration
Challenges those who have will to lead and provides them guidance toward successful leadership of change, renewal and regeneration.

Ken Wessel

It can be done, because it is being done

A developmental journey is a worthwhile, remarkable and stimulating venture that proceeds into the unknown, finds value in discovery and consciously faces and resolves risks involved.

INTRODUCTION

OVERVIEW

BOOK PURPOSE

AUTHORS PERSPECTIVE

DEFINITION OF TERMS

PRINCIPLES OF STAKEHOLDING

STUDY GUIDE

SECTION ONE: GAMES WE PLAY

-CHAPTER LISTING

SECTION TWO: THE WAY FORWARD

-CHAPTER LISTING

CORPORATIONS WITHOUT CONSCIENCE

And Our Responsibility as Would-Be Stakeholders to Cause Them

to Change

Ken Wessel

INTRODUCTION

- Purpose
- Author's perspective

OVERVIEW

- Definition of essential terms (corporate, suppressing, conscience, consciousness, conscientiousness)
- Study guide: using the book
  —structuring concept
  —preciseness in use of words and phrases

PURPOSE OF THIS BOOK

To initiate a process of independent and objective assessment of American Corporations

AS

Powerful machines, primarily intent on satisfying self-interest with indifferent regard for constituent welfare

OR

As living systems dedicated to achieving harmony with their environment and in service to a greater good

SUCH THAT

Employees and other stakeholders are moved to take the lead in causing corporations to aim for fulfillment of their obligation to citizens of the United States who created them, to constructively utilize investments by stakeholders who sustain them, and to conscientiously serve the needs of those who depend on them.

Ken Wessel

This statement of purpose is intended to challenge actual or would-be stakeholders in corporations to take a values based stand in demanding principled corporate behavior with option to withdraw stakes, a more impactful message to corporate officials than any degree of government intervention or moralizing by columnists and others. The net effect is whether corporations continue as self-serving machine-like institutions or dedicate their capabilities to serve a greater good.

AUTHOR'S PERSPECTIVE

It has been a privilege and a unique learning opportunity to work for twenty one years as an employee of Procter & Gamble and three years with SaraLee. I was in a partnership with like-minded others who believed in working together to make a constructive difference, who invested their energy in continuous development of themselves and the organization and were dedicated to creating better tomorrows for the business and its stakeholders.

These corporations as a whole represented by the presence of senior management, stood for lawful and ethical behavior; but most of all insisted on "doing what's right". Policy, rules and audits provided guidance and reinforcement for appropriate conduct in specific situations, but most importantly organization members were expected to be self-accountable for consequences of their actions and self—disciplined in their behavior. A well known principle at P&G, for example; "we will never take advantage of an error by anyone (supplier, customer, employee, community) that is in our favor and against their best interests". I discovered through time that stakeholders of these companies tended to reciprocate with fair and ethical treatment.

These first 24 years of my experience in Corporate America were timely affirmation and reinforcement of values I acquired while growing up on a dairy farm in a farming community whose members invested and tested their values through mutual accountability for welfare of their schools, churches, neighbors, suppliers and customers.

There were of course lapses in correct behavior for which there was a consequence, and adversity that challenged, tested and shaped those values and provided us all with unique opportunities to learn and grow. So I came to P&G at twenty years of age with a BS degree, zero knowledge of corporate life, but with a solid grounding in values and an active conscience to reinforce living by them. During my recruiting visit my values and the

Ken Wessel

values of people with whom I talked were clearly in harmony; the primary factor in accepting the job offer.

During these years my learning, growth and development were enhanced by values for community that brought people together in common effort to work in service to corporation, businesses, stakeholders and fellow employees. There were occasional lapses in behavior that stimulated conscious awareness of consequence and a conscientious attempt to learn from the experience and avoid recurrence. The manner in which well-earned successes were celebrated was also a significant source of learning.

The apex of this learning and personal development came to me through opportunity to be a primary leader in design, construction, startup, operation and expansion of a manufacturing center that is recognized worldwide as the prototype of high performing business systems. This organization is solidly grounded in values for self-managed behavior, teamwork, serving stakeholder needs, zero waste, continuous development, professional excellence, concentration on value adding work, and doing what's right. This organization, the Lima Ohio Manufacturing Center is a modern, industrial expression of lessons I learned from my farming community.

OVERVIEW

PART I: DEFINITION OF TERMS

Following are operational definitions of key terms and phrases. Operational definitions in contrast to Dictionary definitions are intended to enhance our ability to work together with shared meaning of key terms and phrases, knowing that misunderstanding of intended operational meaning derails many interactions.

- **Suppressing Corporate Conscience:** "Removal from one's consciousness by deliberate exclusion of unacceptable thoughts and desires, and forcible prevention of expressions, actions and events that threaten to expose incompetence, weakness and/or unethical behavior".

- **Corporate:** "An entity separate and distinct from owners with rights, responsibilities, and legal and lawful duties, of an individual. Regarded by courts as a fictional, virtual person who can own property, commit crimes and be sued.

- **Modern concept of what a corporation is and what it does:** "Rights of participants and conduct of the enterprise are subject to management discretion. Ownership is separate from management."

Lord Haldane, 1915: "My lords, the corporation is an abstraction. It has no mind of its own any more than it has a body of its own. Its action and direction must consequently be sought in the person of somebody who is really the directing mind and will of the corporation, the very ego and center of the personality of the corporation."

Theodore Roosevelt, first message to congress: "Great corporations exist only because they are created and safeguarded by our institutions; and it is our right and duty to see that they work in harmony with these institutions . . . the first requisite is knowledge, full and complete knowledge which must be made public to the world."

This book will not treat the corporation as a thing or legal artifact, but rather as a living system taking direction and governance from a board of directors, chairman, CEO and senior management, such that they and other employees operate the corporation in response to their dictates. Quality of direction and governance has consequence in terms of success/failure, right/wrong, growth/ decline, etc. Therefore matters of conscience, consciousness and conscientiousness are relevant to actions and behaviors of those who direct the corporation and those who follow that direction. The term "Corporate Officials" will be used throughout the book to include; Board of Directors, Chairman, CEO, COO, CFO, Executive Vice-Presidents (R&D, HR, Engineering, Technical, Legal, PR, etc.), Group Vice-Presidents, VP-General Managers, and individuals who have expert authority sufficient to influence corporate direction and conduct.

Ken Wessel

- **Conscience:** "Awareness of moral or ethical aspect of self-conduct, including the urge to choose right over wrong. A sense of right and wrong that constrains behavior and induces feelings of shame and remorse when its demands are not met".

- **Consciousness:** "Awareness of being aware of existence of a self, knowing its feelings, and ability to make observations of the self". (I know myself objectively and impartially in terms of my thoughts, actions and emotions and recognize the effect of their expression.)

- **Conscientiousness:** "Scrupulous regard for the dictates of conscience. Painstaking, careful, self-disciplined, hard working, reliable, self-directed and thorough in ones efforts on behalf of a greater good".

Experience of these three aspects of behavior can be described as follows; without consciousness the conscience is allowed to sleep, without conscientiousness good intentions go unfulfilled, and without conscience, awareness can express itself in wrong actions. These behavioral issues and stakeholder accountability applies equally to relationships with politicians and media and will be covered in greater detail in Chapter IV.

- **Stakeholder:** Someone who has made an investment in an enterprise and expects a return from it This relationship includes accepting responsibility for how the investment (time, skill, money, materials, etc.) is used. It is irresponsible on the part of a stakeholder to accept misuse of his/her investment by the enterprise including abuse of other stakeholders, so long as "my minimum expectations of return are met" (More on this subject in Chapter I). Change in corporate behavior is not likely to occur without intervention by empowered stakeholders who call corporate officials to account for behaviors that project greed, arrogance, abuse of power and betrayal of obligation to stakeholders. This intervention will likely generate resistance which creates opportunity to surface the underlying issues so they can be resolved.

PART I: PRINCIPLES TO GUIDE STAKEHOLDING RELATIONSHIPS

Even with the best of intentions, behavioral lapses will occur, (as was the case in my farming community and in P&G) therefore it is essential that all parties are consciously aware of and conscientiously aim to be guided by shared principles. The following principles are to be used as guidance for thinking and behavior of stakeholders and corporate officials, to reinforce their aspiration to a purposeful life where skills, resources, assets and energy serve to enrich the life of others.

- Principles are derived from commonly held philosophy and shared values.
- Each party is honor bound to contribute something of value for use by the whole and expects to receive something of value in return.
- Stakeholders value returns that contribute to the welfare of others for whom they are responsible.
- Parties are bonded by complementary relationships.
- Mutual influence is critical in determining best use of asset investment and assessment of fair return.
- Each party is self-accountable for own behavior, accountable for calling attention to behavioral lapses in other parties, and accountable for supporting other parties in correcting behavioral issues.

STUDY GUIDE: USING THE BOOK

Each chapter is generally structured as follows:

- Introduction of subject
- Presentation of issues regarding suppression of conscience
- Description of real life actions that give rise to issues
- Consequence of these actions and who pays the price
- Principles that if followed would avoid these issues
- Reflection questions that you the reader can use to examine and evaluate your relationship with corporations and actions you might take to improve them.

Precise use of words and phrases:

Key words and phrases will be given an operational definition so that we are on the same wave length of arriving at common interpretation of what is intended by statements in the book. Common understanding of intent does not imply agreement but rather that differing opinions will be developed from the same language base.

Failure to arrive at common understanding of key words, phrases and concepts is a technique used by parties to a process of suppressing conscience to avoid confrontation of the issues or to promote a state of denial that they exist. An excruciating example is the common phrase; "XYZ corp. has embarked on a major restructuring" when the real message is they have "*slashed* their payroll by 5000 jobs and imposed spending edicts that have mortgaged the future."

Use of examples to sell an idea, opinion or experience is avoided, although an occasional example is used to illustrate the meaning of a particular point and perhaps add useful content to what you already know. The most useful examples are those drawn from your experience and become a base point for learning. The decision to avoid use of examples is guided by the principle; "transforming knowledge to understanding requires a person to reflect on their experience in a way that integrates elements of knowledge to a level beyond what external teaching can achieve, so that they are able to grasp concepts, relationships and patterns from a variety of viewpoints and come to appreciate the true nature and significance of something."

A fundamental premise on which the book is based is that knowledge alone is insufficient to transform corporations from machine like, self-serving behavior to becoming an open system living in harmony with its environment and working to serve the needs of others. When learning progresses from accumulation of knowledge to acquired understanding, a person is able to see as an integrated whole the motives and motivation that defines their relationship with a corporation, to objectively assess the motives and motivations that guide corporate behavior and to accurately grasp consequence of that relationship.

SECTION ONE: GAMES WE PLAY

Intent of Section One is to issue a wake-up call to all Americans that many, perhaps most corporations, politicians and media are behaving in ways that are destroying historic principles of free enterprise and free markets. The corrosive effects of corporate behavior are not limited to dramatic and highly publicized failures, including Enron, AIG, Bear Stearns, BP, and others, but include lesser known examples of corporate manipulation of enterprise and markets such that they are no longer free. Effects of unconscionable behavior include:

- Draining the economic foundation of America.
- Surrendering vital assets of human skills, technology, products, and systems to other countries.
- Reducing confidence of American People in historic ability to innovate, solve difficult problems, meet significant challenges and invest in the future.
- Fostering climate of political partisanship that creates gridlock in working together for a more desirable future for all Americans.
- Providing media with abundant material they use to promote a cynical and negative outlook for the future of our Country.
- Diminishing the value of leadership and partnering in the conduct of corporate affairs.
- Corporate Officials refers to those with authority to direct corporate behavior and although many behave in concert with core values, sufficient number lack direction by conscience to produce the effects noted above.

We as stakeholders and potential stakeholders in corporations, government, and media have personal responsibility to take a stand on our core values and challenge these institutions to consciously behave according to dictates of conscience, conscientiously serve the needs of all stakeholders and invest in recreating the ideals and principles of free enterprise and free markets. Conclusion of chapters I through XII have a reflective process that aims to draw on our own *experience to provide us with understanding and insights that we can use to make a difference.*

Ken Wessel

CHAPTER LISTING SECTION ONE

Stakeholder betrayal: Benedict Arnold would be proud
An examination of critical nature of living systems as source of value to stakeholders and tendency of many Corporate Officials to establish closed systems to regulate value delivered to stakeholders as means to retain value for self service to own desires.

Stock ownership, impotence and trashing owner's assets
Points out alliance between Wall Street insiders and Corporate Officials that aims to promote self—interest at expense of actual owners/stock holders.

Biting the hand that feeds us
Highlights tactics of corporations that emphasize size and power over suppliers that aim to pressure them to lowest cost and extend special treatment that weakens value chain and reduces value to customers.

Customer beware
Points out collusion between Government and Corporate Officials that not only deny Stakeholders their rights, but also due to lack of conscience ignores doing what is right, giving rise to behavior that ultimately leads to declining values, destruction of free enterprise system and loss in positive spirit of our country.

Sustainability: an exercise of insufficiency
Calls attention to the fact that corporate organizations exist by accident rather than by design and self-serving emphasis on sustaining the physical environment that becomes a fool's errand if the organization itself is not sustainable.

Setting the stage for self-destruction
Exposure of inbuilt flaws that cause Corporate Officials to react unconsciously and obsessively to external threat and adversity, placing welfare of the organization and its stakeholders at risk.

Cost reduction madness: a terminal addiction

Addiction of Corporate Officials to concept that "lean and mean" is attractive to Wall Street, will increase executive control and income and will be tolerated passively by customers and other stakeholders.

Diversity programs: exercise of irony:
Depicts self-serving, cynical and patronizing approach to diversity programs that is self-defeating of fundamental values by assigning people to classes as if their membership was homogeneous, at expense of individual uniqueness.

Empowerment hoax: seduction, coercion, delusion of control
Exposes myth that those in power wish to and are able to empower others.

Job descriptions: pact with the devil
Calls attention to common practice by those in authority of writing job descriptions that impose organization control over the way work is done, impose strict boundaries, and emphasize "nose to the grindstone" approach to work.

Where have all the leaders gone?
Contrasts what effective leaders are and do with behavior of Corporate Officials that undermines and compromises potential for effective leadership.

Self serving motives: Waste without remorse
Active conscience treats waste of any kind as an ultimate taboo, yet Corporate Officials freely waste time, energy, talent and resources in order to serve own desires.

SECTION TWO: THE WAY FORWARD

The intent of Section Two is to advance a practical approach that we as stakeholders can take to reverse the debilitating trend of Corporate, Political and Media institutional behavior described in Section One. In order to realize the potential of thoughts and concepts in Section Two to evoke hope and faith that creating a desirable future is possible and build commitment to work for it, following steps are suggested:
Scan each chapter in turn to get a feel for the material that is presented.

Select elements of the material that spark energy and a desire to make something happen.

Test selected concepts for fit with and support by your experience and potential to enable actions you are considering.

Link with like-minded others in a networking process that aims to engage thoughts of all participants and develop a forward going strategic direction and specific actions that will make it real.

Reach out to others to share your experience as means to expand and extend the effort.

Communicate with Ken Wessel (author) to build on your actions and further energize "The Way Forward."

CHAPTER LISTING: SECTION TWO

I.   Leadership development is the key to a desirable future
     The Leadership Development Forum challenges members of natural work groups to deal with significant real world subjects in real time and to develop an action orientation toward leading team based pursuit of opportunity and resolution of issues, with a sense of urgency and authority.

II. Consciously designed organizations
     It introduces a new perspective on organization design and development that aims to generate continuing research, study, understanding and application so that we use our organizational roles to upgrade design and promote increasing rate of healthy growth.

III. Self-empowerment: choosing our own course in life
     Presents a perspective of empowerment as a natural pursuit for all human beings as we aim for increasing authority, command and control of our everyday affairs and the course of our lives.

IV. Will to become . . . to do . . . to be
     Advances premises about faith, hope, commitment as elements of will to become more of our true self and to live life as a continuously evolving, developing person.

V.   Change, renewal and regeneration

Challenges those who have will to lead and provides them guidance toward successful leadership of change, renewal and regeneration.

VI.   It can be done, because it is being done

A developmental journey is a worthwhile, remarkable and stimulating venture that proceeds into the unknown, finds value in discovery and consciously faces and resolves risks involved

Ken Wessel

CHAPTER I

BENEDICT ARNOLD WOULD BE PROUD

Corporate Betrayal of Stakeholders

STAKEHOLDING

Stake-holding in a business enterprise is a process that includes these elements:

1. A person or organization makes a free will investment (stake) of something of personal value, in an enterprise for use by the enterprise to pursue its ends. *This is the activating force in stake-holding. Without these investments the enterprise lacks the means for survival or success.*

2. The investor has legitimate reason to expect a fair return on investment from the enterprise. *This is the restraining force in stake-holding. Without expectation of fair return potential stakeholders will withdraw or reduce their stake and hold it or invest it elsewhere.* Effect on the enterprise is to reduce access to means required for success.

3. In a healthy system of stake-holding the enterprise and its stakeholders share influence over how stakes will be used and fair return determined. *This is the reconciling force in stake-holding. Without this partnership the relationship tends to degrade to a point where each party aims to serve own interest at expense of the other if necessary.*

4. Corporate officials are deaf and blind to sharing influence with stakeholders, and in fact view them as parasites, feeding on corporate success. Therefore stakeholders are dismissed as not consequential to success of a business enterprise.

Ken Wessel

OPEN AND CLOSED SYSTEMS

We will look at stakeholding in the context of open systems theory, a subset of general systems theory posed by Ludwig von Bertallanfy. Open systems are those with capacity to create life and sustain it through a wide range of environmental circumstances. Closed systems on the other hand, are at the mercy of forces in their environment and are controlled by the law of entropy.

The first requirement of an open (living) system is to establish a boundary interface that defines it as separate from its environment. It is across this interface that it transacts with stakeholders and other systems. With stakeholders, transactions will be measured by exchange of value, preferably based on a partnership. Nature of relationship with other systems determines the medium of transaction and can include; master/ slave, competitive, adversarial, hostile/warlike, paternalistic, philanthropic, contractual, partnership, etc.

In absence of a boundary a system does not exist, it has become part of the surrounding environment and has no independent identity. When Eastern Airlines disappeared into bankruptcy and was dissolved as a discrete entity, its assets, materials, employees, trademarks, cash; routes, gates, etc. were absorbed by a host of other, living systems. When the membrane/ boundary of a living system cell ruptures, the cell dies and its contents are either absorbed and utilized by neighboring living cells or neutralized and discarded as waste to be utilized by a still larger environment. It is the nature of eco-systems to utilize all materials as potential components of living systems

The second requirement for open systems is capability to operate a value adding process that imports materials (natural resources, goods, services, ideas, information) from the environment and transforms them in such a way that outputs of greater value are exported to the environment. For example; a wedding gown is of greater value to the bride than fibers it is made from; functional software means more to a computer operator than the array of 1's and 0's that were inputs to creating it. The essence of stakeholder relationships is based on achieving harmony in this exchange of value such that needs of the enterprise and its stakeholders are met and waste of all kind is minimized.

The implosion of Eastern Airlines was due to a perfect storm of stakeholders withdrawing their stakes.

Union refused to allow employees to rally in support of the Corporation, major stockholders demanded a greater return than was possible leading to a sharp drop in share price, customers were untrusting of schedules, reliability and safety, and communities were weary of uncertainty about the corporations future and ready to move on to a more healthy airline system. As stakeholders withdrew, non-stakeholder entities were on the attack, protecting their self-interest, including unions, a host of government agencies, creditors and competitors.

A third requirement of open systems is that they sustain a process of healthy growth and development that is internally generated, supported by systems in the environment, and synchronized with their evolution. Open systems expand boundaries through time, becoming more self-sufficient and increasingly interdependent with the environment. Successful investment in development is the only means to reverse effects of the law of entropy; the inbuilt tendency of systems toward disorganization, rundown and decay. Maintenance alone and incremental improvement are insufficient; development is required to move the system to sustainably higher levels of purpose, capability and state.

Procter & Gamble has existed as a living system since 1837 largely due to excellence in solving problems, creative approaches to continuous improvement, and most of all the will of capable leaders to change products, technology and the organization. A leading example is the decision to enter the liquid laundry detergent market causing a likely decline in powdered detergents where P&G dominated the market. Result is that the combined share of laundry detergent markets has expanded, all stakeholders have benefited from the change and reinforced their stake, and the historic pattern of corporate evolution has been extended.

Capability of a system to sustain life through time in a dynamic environment depends on management of the boundary interface in a way that requires minimum investment of attention, energy and resources while importing elements of value and excluding contaminants. Valuable imports include useful knowledge, necessary supplies, contractor support, support from trade groups, etc. Contaminants include attraction to external recognition, attacks on reputation, litigation, etc. Contaminants and environmental threat require the system to divert attention, energy and resources from its value adding process to boundary maintenance at risk of a reduced return to stakeholders. In the event of an extremely hostile environment a system must move to a more supportive environment in order to sustain its life.

It is in the interest of corporations who value stakeholder partnerships as a critical success factor in their part of the world to offer stakeholders the best overall deal. Employee stakeholders universally accept that corporate investment in their training and development is an important element of return for what they have invested and at the same time corporation enjoys the benefit of an enhanced employee investment. Therefore, arbitrary elimination of training and development activities as a cost reduction technique appears to be an action devoid of consciousness, conscientiousness and conscience. (Ref: chapter; "Self Destructive Impulse of Modern Organizations.")

BETRAYAL OF STAKEHOLDER INTERESTS

During the nineteenth century the label "Robber Baron" was use to describe business men who dominated the market place and stakeholders by use of illegal, unethical and unfair business practices in order to amass power, control and fortune. For them, influence of conscience was an obvious non issue.

The term, Robber Baron was coined to describe illegal charging of tolls by medieval German royalty.

"Captains of Industry" is a twentieth century term that softened the concept of Robber Baron, but referred to the same behavior.

Behavior of corporations over the past century as represented by corporate officials led to the creation of a host of third parties who presume to represent each class of their stakeholders. Third parties presume to represent stakeholder interests as they intervene with corporations on behalf of stakeholders.

Presence of a third party creates at least two more boundaries between corporation and stakeholder, each of which consumes valuable energy and resources and diverts attention from value adding work.

Third parties have their own interest to serve which siphons additional value from the relationship between corporation and stakeholder. Because quality of employee stakeholding is a life and death matter for corporations it will be treated in this chapter and other stakeholders in following chapters.

A century ago in the U.S., employees were routinely forced to work extra hours without pay and prior notice. Working conditions were a constant threat to life and limb and long-term health. Resistance meant loss of job and at times industry blacklisting. Corporations often took credit for employee improvement ideas and in many cases employees were discouraged from working for improvement. After decades of maltreatment, international labor unions were formed to present a strong and united force to resist behavior of those who represent and speak for the corporation.

CORPORATE MANAGEMENT AND UNIONS:
TWO CLOSED SYSTEMS

Virtually all corporations via directors and senior management have viewed employees through the lens of "management rights", which legitimized treatment that ranged from outright abuse to extremes of paternalism. Those who abused corporate power created an employee work experience that was unsatisfying at best and often debilitating of mind, spirit and body did so:

- By taking a stand on management rights without concern for what is right and what is wrong

- In a mechanical fashion without feeling or objectivity

- By working to satisfy self-serving motives

Clearly, corporate abuse of employees sets a limit on a stakeholding relationship and can reduce it to its most materialistic level, 8 hours time for 8 hours pay and no upsets. The immediate effect is to establish a ceiling on employee and organization performance and value of its outputs. This in turn reduces return potential for other stakeholders; customers, society, owners and suppliers. They in order to maintain themselves as an open system will look to other organizations as investment opportunities with higher level returns.

A corporation with sufficient degree of consciousness will notice the negative effect as employees withdraw their stakes and take steps to change their behavior. This is the point where conscience becomes critical. When a shift in employee treatment is only a technique to rescue the business and is not based on doing what's right; people will catch on to the hypocrisy and limit their investment to match what is a guaranteed return. And until the organization is willing to share influence, the stakeholding relationship will never reach its potential.

Opportunity for the corporation to make even minor improvements in employee stakeholding is typically lost when employees form a labor union. *The union based on its own purpose is not a stakeholder in the corporation and employees are required to withdraw elements of their stakeholding in the corporation in order to support union purposes.* The union has nothing of value to invest in the business and the business has no intent to provide a return. Therefore, the legal, contractual, and cross purposed nature of union-management relationships insure that neither party will freely contribute to the health and welfare of the other. Furthermore, since the union has no process for transforming inputs to outputs of value to the environment, its existence depends on drawing energy, materials and resources from other systems, primarily business, its members and society/government. It is a classic example of a closed system, essentially a parasite regardless of whether it is passive or aggressive. And as a parasite it is certain to influence systems it feeds on to move toward themselves becoming closed systems. (Parasite: "One who lives at the expense of others without making any useful return.")

The parasitic process attacks the essence of what creates and sustains life in an open system by disrupting the even exchange of value between the enterprise and its other stakeholders. Attention and resources involved in combating the union are diverted from the life giving task of creating and exporting value. This will reduce fair return needed and expected by all stakeholders (including employees) who in turn will have reason to withdraw at least a portion of their investment, further limiting enterprise capability to serve stakeholder interest . . . a classic example of entropy at work. Continuing struggle with unions at the boundary/interface tends to render it weak and fragile as other systems (competitors, government agencies, groups in the community) may choose to take advantage of the situation to further their own self-interest or to become isolated out of concern for being drawn into the fray.

Corporations typically intensify their stand on "management rights" when engaging the union and adopt a warlike position (declared or undeclared.) Consequence of this attitude is predictable:

- Union responds in kind and mounts strongest possible defense and/or counterattack

- Corporation shifts attention, energy and resources from the life-giving process of creating value

Corporation tends to reduce or eliminate investment in developing capability of its employees due to negative energy in the environment, desire to reduce expense, growing isolation of employees and doubt of their loyalty.
Employees are often caught in a no man's land between union and management and run the risk of becoming collateral damage. Employees who are also union officials can become specific targets for management reprisal. In any case level of employee stakeholding is diminished.

RECREATING OPEN SYSTEM

The collective of Corporate Officials may relate to their stakeholders and their environment at different levels of awareness. If their tendency is to be arrogant and ignorant they will likely operate from old habits and not notice that employees are bailing out, in revolt, or joining unions until the damage is irreversible. When they become sensitive to employee issues a typical response is to create an illusion that employee needs are recognized. This attitude gives rise to employee of the month awards, ice—cream and cake celebrations, recreational activities, employee committees to work on better meal and break area options, etc. This approach became institutionalized as the Quality of Work Life movement and the formation of Quality Circles. When employees discovered there was no real increase in shared influence these and similar movements died out.

When however Corporate Officials become objectively conscious of their behavior toward employees and unions as measured by right vs. wrong and its consequence in terms of harm to the corporation and other stakeholders, *and who experience regret relative to that behavior,* they are in a position to regenerate their stakeholding relationship with employees. Key points in engaging employees:

- Approach them as colleagues who control unique and essential talent, skill, and qualities of potential value as investments in the corporations businesses.

- Engage in open dialogue to explore specific investments employees are willing and able to make, what would constitute a fair return on each level of investment and terms of a partnership approach to manage administration of investment and returns.

- Invest in training and development of employees and the organization as an integrated effort. (Growth and development are a third element essential to the life of a system.)

- Establish and live by mutually held principle; "no role will be created or staffed to do non productive work." This principle supports the work ethic that employees aspire to, focuses employee assets on value adding work, and prevents massive, mandated reductions in force.

- Avoid discussion of subjects that are off limits per union-management contract or labor law and any reference to union-management relationships.

Employee stakeholders freely invest their time, effort, energy, skill, ingenuity, and creativity in order to operate the transformation process at high levels of effectiveness and efficiency on a daily basis while improving and renewing it through time. The business recognizes employees as a unique and independent system with legitimate needs and aims to fulfill those needs with fair return on employee investment. Forms of fair return include satisfying material and security needs, recognition for making a constructive difference, contributing to personal growth and development, and creating a culture of belonging.

Employees are unique among stakeholders in that they exist as independent systems in the corporate environment and at the same time as indispensable parts of the corporate whole. Therefore, corporations whose representatives treat employees as property ("employees are our most important assets") restrict access to the full range of what employees have capacity to invest.

Business and its employees realize that achieving maximum value of employee investment and the spirit of fair return will depend on shared influence in determining how investment is best used and the components of fair return. Neither party isolated from the other is able to know or understand the necessary dimensions of wise investing or fair return.

As stakeholders or would-be stakeholders we must beware of falling into the role of enabler; "One who supplies the means to make something feasible or operational." Using means at our disposal to promote actions or behavior that are just plain wrong, with intent to serve our own ends, ought to be an issue for our conscience to wrestle with.

Following are a number of principles (adapted from writings of Immanuel Kant) to guide us as we work to generate appropriate behavior by Corporate Officials and all other organization members.

- When enough people collectively behave immorally or unethically, so called current accepted practice becomes meaningless.

- Stakeholders have value that transcends price and cannot ethically be used as an element of cost to satisfy corporate financial self-interest.

- Controlling others via coercion, seduction or deception reduces them to level of a tool.

- Conversely, respect for humanity as ends, requires contribution to development of their innate capacity.

- People have a right to open, available and relevant information that they need to manage their work and personal affairs.

Ken Wessel

PERSONAL REFLECTION

Following are questions that all employees should ask of themselves as well as those of us whose ability to function as sustainable, living systems is threatened by corporate behavior:

Q1: As an employee (or other) stakeholder what talent, skill, commitment to value adding work, resources at my command, innovative capability and undeveloped potential are consciously available for me to invest in _____corporation if I choose to do so?

Q2: In what way might the corporation use my investment to achieve its ends?

Q3: What would be a reasonable return for each level of investment in terms of fairness and meeting my needs as they escalate through time and in proportion to my investment?

Q4: Is there reason to believe that my view of reasonable return would be resisted by the corporation?

Q5: Is there reason to believe that my investment would be used unwisely or counterproductively?

Q6: What is my responsibility to create and use influence to move the corporation toward effective use of what I am willing to invest and agreement to fair return?

Q7: What steps might I take to exercise my responsibility?

CHAPTER I

BENEDICT ARNOLD WOULD BE PROUD

CORPORATE BETRAYAL OF STAKEHOLDERS

Ken Wessel

CHAPTER II

STOCK OWNERSHIP, IMPOTENCE AND TRASHING OWNERS ASSETS

Corporate Betrayal of Stakeholders

OWNER AS STAKEHOLDER

A simplistic view of owners (shareholders/stockholders) is of those who invest money to purchase shares for which they are paid dividends. In modern times the promise of stock appreciation has eclipsed dividends as the form of return most valued by owners. Exercise of mutual influence (between owners and corporate officials) is almost unheard of; unilateral decisions by Corporate Officials set dividend rates and the stock market establishes share price.

Stockholders own the assets of the corporation which may increase or decrease in value through time but which in fact play an insignificant role in providing return to owners.

OWNERS AND IMPOTENCE

Corporate officials focus their attention on the denizens of Wall Street ("insiders frequently found at a particular place"); fund managers, brokers, analysts, investment bankers and business press and go to great lengths to gain their favor and leave the actual owners to fend for themselves. Owners have legal right to vote their shares at annual meetings but have a well established record of rare success in going against management proposals and recommendations.

Owners stand by helplessly as Corporate Officials engage in a ritualistic dance with power figures from Wall Street. They dance to the beat of:

- Forecast annual and quarterly earnings that set the stage for financial and psychological betrayal of common sense management of financial affairs.

- Profit warnings issued when corporation expects to miss or exceed forecast and which can have the effect of sending a shock wave through the market.

- "Buy-hold-sell" and other forms of analyst advice that energize share movement and income to Wall Street firms, who are paid by the buy-sell transaction and not for performance.

- Cost cutting and downsizing campaigns arbitrarily mandated by Corporate Officials with expectation of an upward bump in share price and easy profits to come.

- Stock option awards to Corporate Officials based on share price appreciation regardless of effect on future viability of the corporation and security of its employees.

A warning shot was fired across owners bow when a Fortune Magazine cover featured top CEO's ranked exclusively on share price appreciation without regard for dividends, or long term projection of growth and health of the corporation.

Employees who are also owners via 401K and stock purchase plans and have pensions based on stock ownership are in the unenviable position of being doubly victimized. In each situation fund managers or trustees make decisions that have profound financial impact with little influence from employee/owners.

Owners are limited to three possible decisions; "buy-sell-hold" and beyond that have no influence on utilizing assets they own to achieve maximum return on their investment. Stockholder revolt of the 60's and 70's (Agent Orange, doing business in South Africa, industrial-military complex) are not even a distant memory and offer no direction or hope to today's owners nor warning to Corporate Officials.

Issues of lack of consciousness (knowing about the status of owners) repressed conscience (caring about their welfare) and lax conscientiousness (due diligence in working for long term benefit of owners) abound in most corporations for reasons previously noted. Egregious abuse of owners by Enron, WorldCom,

Adelphia and others generated lots of smoke but no fire of reform. If anything, those who call the tune in the shareholder dance have perfected their process, reduced risk of legal issues and sharpened the definition between what is unlawful and what is merely unethical. The collapse of major Wall Street firms and others in the mortgage business is clear and shocking testimony to the self-serving motives of many corporations, ultimately betrayed by their arrogance and ignorance.

Generations ago, corporate abuse of owners led to formation of the Security and Exchange Commission whose role was to protect the interests of owners from abuse by corporations and Wall Street. The SEC in much the same way as labor unions, is not a stakeholder and has the same characteristics of a parasite, (on continuous life support by taxpayers, have made no useful investment of value, and avoid partnerships based on mutual influence.) To make matters worse they are not a reliable parasite, are understaffed, poorly organized and have stood on the sidelines while the economy and owner welfare went into a downward spiral.

TRASHING OWNERS ASSETS

Assets are elements of the Corporation that act on materials such that materials are transformed from specified input values to output products of greater value (value adding process) measured by their ability to meet stakeholder judgment of how well their needs are served. Input materials include base chemicals, natural resources (crude oil, air, water, metals, soil, etc.), information, ideas/thinking, etc.

Assets are not used up in the transformation, do not become part of the product, but may wear out with extended use and lack of maintenance. Assets include equipment that manipulates material, people skills that enable effective management of other assets, and systems that optimize the work of all other assets. For example, reactors, mixers, cooling and heating devices, etc. cause raw materials to change form as desired until finished product specifications are achieved. These assets perform at peak potential when they are managed by operators who willingly apply the asset value of their skill and who are supported by assets in the form of systems (scheduling, preventive maintenance, quality control) that optimize asset management effectiveness.

Infrastructure, good will, and reputation are assets that have a role in maintaining a healthy interface with the environment so that the value adding process is free to fulfill its purpose.

Supplies that are neither asset nor part of product output include copy paper, energy to operate HVAC, lubricants, etc. These consumables ought to be top priority for cost reduction efforts.

Assets may be acquired, developed, maintained at status quo, allowed to run down or divested.

Corporate abuse of assets can be seen at each of these levels. Following are perspectives on how each level of asset management ought to be approached, contrasted with forms of mismanagement by Corporate Officials because:

- They are unconsciously ignorant of the relationship between asset management and long term health, growth and viability of the enterprise.

- Short term, self serving motives blind their conscience to wasteful, sometimes immoral/unethical behavior toward asset management. In all cases they fail in fiduciary duty to act as stewards of owner/shareholders property.

- They lack the level of conscientious effort required to think through optimum approach to Asset management, to formulate long and short term plans for executing that approach and to follow-up with the organization to see that plans are faithfully carried out.

Acquisition of assets ought to be based on making a conscious investment in creating a better future for the corporation and its stakeholders.

Investment thinking would consider a reasonable rate of return based on increased product value resulting from more effective and efficient value adding process operations that newly acquired assets make possible.

Acquisition of assets is restrained and the future is mortgaged when Corporate Officials:

- Roll back capital investments in order to "make the numbers."

- Impose a hiring freeze in order to reduce fixed cost.

- Purchase assets in response to lowest cost (sourcing view) vs. overall value in use (operators view) leading to poor ROI and discouraging further investment.

- Ignore threat from competitor investment in assets because effect will not have immediate impact.

Development of assets refers to change in potential contribution of assets by investing in their capability to serve a larger purpose, function with greater efficiency and effectiveness and sustain a higher state of performance (more reliable, more safe, less polluting.)

Development of assets is compromised when Corporate Officials:

- Impose cost cutting rules that prohibit access to expertise that is capable of leading and guiding developmental efforts and deny use of resources required to activate new developments.

- Allow asset designs to become obscure and the state of assets to rundown to point where change and development lack an adequate base to build on.

- Recognize and reward fire-fighting (duct tape and baling wire) approach to keeping assets on line vs. the longer term benefits of asset acquisition and development. Rewards for fire-fighting undermine value for establishing performance standards and rigorously living up to them.

- Ignore the principle; "the only continuously developmental asset of any organization is the quality of thinking of its members."

Maintaining assets at status quo is based on a myth that an asset can be held at its nameplate condition despite ordinary wear and tear, effect of entropy and change in its operating environment. When Corporate Officials adopt this position it signals that they have bought the myth, are willing to gamble that stakeholder needs remain static and competition will not invest in asset upgrade.

Rundown of assets is based on an illusion that assets fully paid for or depreciated can be allowed to run out their useful life for free. What Corporate Officials fail to understand is that these underperforming assets reduce output of the value adding process and value delivered to stakeholders. Although these assets may be paid for in depreciation terms they require more than optimum share of maintenance, investment of additional energy, added attention from operators, and risk failure at most inconvenient time.

Divesting an asset occurs when the corporation surrenders ownership and obligation for asset stewardship. Corporate Officials fail this step when principles and conditions for divestiture are not clear and followed and unused assets are allowed to continue to incur expense even though removed from use.

THINKING AND BEHAVIORAL FLAWS
OF CORPORATE OFFICIALS

The phrase "employees are our most important asset" is exposed as a patronizing untruth when training and development are banned in order to reduce cost, causing a decline in asset value of employee skill and challenges their will to make maximum contribution. This attitude is reinforced by accounting practices that classify all costs associated with employees as an item of expense which plays into a mindset; "reducing expense is always good for the business." If employee skills willingly invested in support of the business were viewed as an asset, cost associated with acquiring developing and maintaining the asset could be justified.

Outsourcing is a common ploy of Corporate Officials who aim to realize an immediate reduction in expense by contracting for lower wage labor. This action is a clear sign that they do not in fact view employees as "our most important asset," that they lack the will and skill to invest in acquiring or developing these assets, and they are willing to mortgage the future for short term personal gains.

Declaration by Corporate Officials that our top priority is; "creation of shareholder value" is a statement of extreme hypocrisy. This becomes apparent when a rundown of assets (real property of owners) is mandated in order to pump up the share price bubble which results in a paper gain for owners but a loss in value of what they own, an immediate financial gain for Corporate Officials in the form of stock options and increased business revenue for Wall Street.

The denizens of Wall Street can be accurately classified as parasites because they make no investment in the corporation, seek maximum financial gain for themselves without regard for stakeholder interests or long term health and viability of the enterprise, and become expert manipulators of the corporation through their relationship with Corporate Officials who become expert enablers of Wall Street excesses.

PERSONAL REFLECTION

Some organizations live by the principle; "the only continuously improvable asset of any organization is the capacity of its people to self-generate increasing quality of their thinking," Quality of thinking simply means; "thinking that is fit for use in terms of the actions and behavior it produces." For example, thinking that fails to base decisions on consideration of consequence is not fit for use. And thinking that produces a viable philosophy for what the organization is to become creates a developmental context for thinking and behavior that ultimately leads to actions that create a viable future.

Following are questions that all owner/stockholders should ask of themselves as well as those of us whose ability to function as a living system is threatened by corporate behavior.

Q1: What have I invested in ____ corporation? Does it matter if I know who I have invested in?

Q2: If I have only invested money, what is my reaction to the way the corporation treats its customers, employees and the larger community?

Q3: As an owner, what is my responsibility toward how my assets are being used and the effect they produce?

Q4: What steps might I/should I take to exert necessary influence to insure that my assets are being used in a way that reflects my principles and values?

Ken Wessel

CHAPTER II

STOCK OWNERSHIP, IMPOTENCE AND TRASHING

OWNERS ASSETS CORPORATE BETRAYAL OF

STAKEHOLDERS

CHAPTER III

BITING THE HAND THAT FEEDS US

Suppliers: Often a Case of Indentured Servitude

SUPPLY

An operational definition of supply: "To furnish to someone what is needed." Suppliers are the source of materials that are transformed into outputs that provide fair return to stakeholders and are critical to the life of any organization

A value chain begins with original sources that enter the chain because of the actions of a supplier. This supplier transacts with a customer who becomes a supplier to another customer and so on. Value chains continue through end users and ultimately recycle (in chains that adhere to principles of sustainable natural resources.)

If any element of the value chain dies or declines toward closed system behavior the entire chain is at risk. (Value chain is no better than its weakest link.) Replacing or renovating a defective link limits capability of each element to continuously meet stakeholder value needs therefore each element of the chain has a stake in maintaining the health of other elements.

CUSTOMER INITIATED ISSUES FOR SUPPLIERS

- "We're the customer they need/owe us."

- Cut throat bidding (law of the jungle) where customer leaks status of bidding process to play one supplier against another.

- Threats to terminate relationship.

- Low cost bidder is our friend regardless of overall value delivered. Organization structures that link a buyer who may be rewarded by holding down cost with a sales person who may be rewarded by increasing volume, leads to a relationship based on price. Accepting materials that do not meet value requirements of input to value adding process requires customer to cut corners and ultimately reduce value output to its customers, contaminating the entire chain.

- Boundaries become fortresses based on defensive legal language and positions.

- Failure to establish clear, mutually agreed to performance specifications, quality standards and customer service expectations, leads to low trust, intensive auditing of transactions and bias to frequent claims.

- "If we help supplier to improve they might take that improvement to our competitor." This attitude is also at expense of a healthy, growing value chain.

EGREGIOUS EXAMPLE

This example is excerpted from customer and business writer's assessment of actions and behavior of

Jose Lopez, Purchasing VP for General Motors in the early '90's. His approach to suppliers included:

- Aiming for multiple bids on first round of bidding; some bids were solicited without intent to buy and some bids were fictitious.

- Initiating a second round of bidding beginning with low first round bid as ceiling. Suppliers were overtly played off one another.

- Winning bidder was often pressured to agree to further cost reductions and contract was at times torn up to force negotiation of a better one; for GM.

Effects of this approach include:

- Alienation of long term suppliers.

- Withdrawal and shutdown of some suppliers.

- Shift from partner relationships to reinforced boundaries based on legalism.

- Contracts lost real meaning.

- Ford became alarmed for fear that shared component suppliers would go out of business and further depress the US auto industry.

SIGNS OF HOPE

A number of corporate officials have recognized healthy supplier relationships as a source of competitive advantage and a potential source of increasing value returns to stakeholders. This shift begins as a matter of enlightened self-interest that will hopefully extend to understanding and value for establishing open systems throughout the value chain.

They are working to establish healthy boundary/interface relationships. When suppliers and customers are linked in a partnership relationship they reduce the amount of energy, resources and attention required to maintain their interface and increase what is available to increase value that flows through the value chain.

PERSONAL REFLECTION

Select a corporation who is an important personal supplier and/or a key supplier to your company.

Q1: How well has their product performed in terms of living up to; specifications, quality standards, customer service promises and price that is both fair and affordable?

Q2: What are actual examples of where supplier does/does not meet your needs and expectations?

Q3: How do you see your responsibility to provide accurate performance feedback to selected suppliers?

Q4: What are essential elements in developing a supplier-customer relationship that benefits both parties?

Q5: What next steps will you take?

CHAPTER III

BITING THE HAND THAT FEEDS US

SUPPLIERS: OFTEN A CASE OF INDENTURED

SERVITUDE

CHAPTER IV

CAVEAT EMPTOR: BUYER BEWARE

Extracting Value From Customers
and Other Stakeholders

STAKEHOLDING

Employees are the source of human energy and asset value of applied skills that do vital work:

- Effective and efficient management of value adding processes of their organization.

- Maintenance of a healthy, robust and expansive boundary/ interface with entities in the environment.

- Creating a desirable future.

Owners are the vital source of capital required to acquire, maintain and improve assets.

Suppliers are the source of indispensible inputs to the value adding process.

Customer, also known as client, buyer, purchaser of goods and services of a supplier or seller. "Customer" is derived from "custom" meaning one who is expected to continue as a purchaser.

Customer is the only reliable source of revenue that is economic fuel for the supplier's value adding process.

Therefore without a continuing flow of cash from customers, supplier system is destined for life support, or death.

Customer as stakeholder ought to expect as a minimum return product values that; perform up to specifications, achieve stated quality standards, deliver prompt and responsive customer service, and are fairly and affordably priced. For this customers invest prompt and full payment of selling price.

When customer-supplier relationship is based on shared influence, characteristic of a partnership; corporate officials abstain from partnerships believing that they increase vulnerability and call for shared influence that leads to benefits for each party.

- Customer can make plans for present and invest in future confident that supplier promises to deliver products of specified value will be met.

- Therefore customers are more able to achieve their potential for growth and development, and contribute to value chain health that benefits customer and supplier alike.

- Healthy customers are a more reliable source of investment in suppliers system, enabling supplier's

- Confidence in plans for short and long term. Again, the value chain and each part of it benefits.

At a higher level of stakeholding customers can invest constructive feedback or suggestions for product improvements or active promotion of supplier's products. In return a customer can expect higher value products and more responsive supplier behavior. Customer-supplier partnership is means for reconciling higher order investment with expectation of higher value returns.

CUSTOMER BEWARE OF:

- Supplier systems of non accountability lead to stonewalling, dead ends, or foot-dragging in response to complaints. Insurance companies have become expert practitioners of the "wear them down until they give up" process.

- Lobbyists that compromise safeguards against customer abuse by bringing pressure to bear on legislators and regulators. (FDA decisions that go against unanimous position of expert advisors.)

- Manipulation of purchase decisions through seductive, deceptive and misleading advertising. (Big Pharma is locked in to this approach.)

- Price fixing (airlines are usual suspects.)

- Monopolistic practices. (Excessive fares by airline that commands high percentage of flights from a particular airport.)

- Deceptive packaging (contents do not match picture on box, excessive unused volume, etc.)

- Claims based on "fake science," (Herbal supplements.)

These are among the usual examples of supplier willingness to serve self by taking advantage of customers.

DECLINING CORE VALUES OF A ONCE GREAT NATION

However the real issues that relate to "caveat emptor" are far more serious and account for a continuing and pervasive decline among citizens of the United States in:

- Integrity of moral fabric
- everyday spirit of optimism and hopefulness
- fruitless search for partnering across boundaries
- will to take a stand on principles and call the Federal Government and corporate executives to account for their behavior and to pay the price for their failings
- factual knowledge of everyday truth and reality
- shifting toward emotion as stimulus for action while discounting value of intellect
- receptivity to influence by self-serving biased media, partisan politicians, and self-anointed experts

As citizens we are customers of supplier corporations who provide goods and services and also consumers of laws created by Congress, administration of law by the Executive Branch and Mediation by the Judiciary.

We as a nation are paying a daily price and compromising our future by accepting and even enabling a vast conspiracy between Corporate America and the Federal Government, most notably hijacking the Congress of

The United States. The overpowering influence of Corporate America is exponentially increased by banding together in trade associations and special interest groups including; NRA, AARP. phRMA, NMA, Chambers of Commerce, etc.

Commerce; API, Business Round Table, World Economic Forum, and hundreds of others.

The alarm was sounded by President Eisenhower in his 1961 farewell speech:

"My fellow Americans;

. . . . In the councils of government, we must guard against the acquisition of unwarranted influence, whether sought or unsought, by the military-industrial complex. The potential for the disastrous rise of misplaced power exists and will persist. We must never let the weight of this combination endanger our liberties or democratic processes. We should take nothing for granted. Only an alert and knowledgeable citizenry can compel the proper meshing of the huge industrial and military machinery of defense with our peaceful methods and goals, so that security and liberty may prosper together."

AN UNCONSCIOUSLY INCOMPETENT
FEDERAL GOVERNMENT

Unconscious incompetence includes elements of a state that; denies reality, seeks to embellish the status quo, avoids self-improvement, feeds on its own arrogance, and is trending from illusion to delusion. It is characterized by the fable; "The Emperor has no Clothes," and illustrated by these examples:

- Faux expression of surprise at illegal behavior by Halliburton and KBR in theft of taxpayer dollars

- SEC sleeping on the job while Bernie looted citizens of $50B+

- "Good job Brownie"

- "Mission accomplished"

- Belief that massive increases in ethanol production from corn (as promoted by Big Ag) will ease dependence on foreign oil, and improve the environment without creating negative consequence greater than expected benefits. In fact, lobbyists for a variety of corporate interests (big oil, auto industry and suppliers, traders in petroleum stocks, real estate interests etc. have conspired to maintain dependence on foreign oil.

- And many more similar examples

INACTIVE CONSCIENCE IN CORPORATE: FEDERAL GOVERNMENT RELATIONSHIP

Corporations and their Congressional allies (true of most, but not all) are blind and deaf to expressions of shame, remorse, regret, embarrassment and other manifestations of conscience.

Sophisticated forms of self-defense, justification, and rationalization support extensions of unconscionable behavior, deception and camouflage but seldom result in correction. For example;

- The World Economic Forum at Davos presents itself as an opportunity for presentation and debate of global economic issues (which has not lead to sustainable constructive action) but is in reality cover for Corporate Executives to engage high level political figures in creating business deals.

- Member organizations of phRMA make public offers to help financially strapped customers with partial payment for prescription drugs and have offered to add money to Medicare D, while their trade association (phRMA):

-Is spending an estimated $1.2M/day lobbying for favorable treatment by federal government, including defeat of health care reform legislation.

-Was able to lobby passage of Medicare part D that greatly expanded the market for prescription drugs while prohibiting Medicare from negotiating for lower prices, therefore creating taxpayer funding of huge increases in member company profits.

-Was defending double digit increases in prescription drug cost as being due to R&D expense even though marketing expense is nearly double R&D.

- American Petroleum Institute has formed a consortium "Energy Citizens" whose aim is to fight climate change legislation. The consortium includes dozens of companies in the energy industry, American

Farm Bureau, American Conservative Union, Freedom Works, and many others. Their strategy includes hiring and training bloggers and forming so-called grass roots rallies to attack climate change and industry regulatory efforts (seeming to be independent of API control.) They have published wide spread and now discredited claims that climate change legislation will lead to sky rocketing energy costs and loss of 2M+ jobs. To their credit Shell has withdrawn from participation in rallies and have announced a desire to take a leading role in climate change improvement.

"American Health Insurance Plans" is the lobbying front for a consortium of insurance companies whose announced aim is to "administer a knockout punch to health care legislation." Their biased and flawed study that showed Baucus Bill would increase health care cost has been widely discredited as blatantly self-serving. Again, individual companies have announced support for health care reform while using their lobbying front to serve their real aims.

The list goes on and on and as citizens we must take time and diligent effort to search for truth behind lobbying fronts and take active and affirming positions that expose failures of conscience and hypocrisy of businesses that demonstrate this behavior.

A SATANIC MARRIAGE: FAILURES OF CONSCIENCE AND CONSCIENTEOUSNESS

A number of businesses have found a way to create a "black hole of misery, despair and economic hardship" for all classes of stakeholder; employees, customers, owners, suppliers and society. Following are groups of business organizations and Federal Government bodies that are implicated in a wide ranging conspiracy that has created this black hole; some of whom contributed only through unconscious incompetence while others were driven by greed, thirst for fame and power and were unchecked by any degree of conscience or conscientious sense of duty or due diligence. Ratio of executive pay to that of other employees has grown to an indefensible display of greed, power, and demonstration of arrogant superiority.

- Corporate business organizations; Enron, Tyco, World Com, Adelphia, ImClone, Madoff, and others.

- Wall Street Firms and banks; Goldman Sachs, Merrill Lynch, Lehman Brothers, AIG, Countrywide

Financial, Bear Stearns, Bank of America, Citigroup, Salomon Brothers, Freddie Mac, Fannie Mae, and others.

- Audit and accounting firms; Arthur Anderson, KPMG, Deloitte & Touche, PricewaterhouseCoopers, and others, who cooked books to enhance reputation of their clients.

- Credit and debt rating agencies; Moody's, Standard and Poors, and others, that hyped credit levels to cause stakeholders to support failing businesses.

- Federal Government; SEC, FTC, FCC, FDA, and other enforcement agencies were generally asleep at the switch and stripped of vital resources by congress who also failed to exercise oversight of federal agencies and business organizations who were egregiously failing their stakeholders.

- The Supreme Court denied investor lawsuits against Wall Street Banks who defrauded/failed their investors.

- Media in all forms pursued their own self-interest of sales volume, ratings and pandering to demographic expectations at the expense of serving public interest via accurate, timely, objective and fearless search for and reporting of essential truth.

Sadly, this conspiracy has manipulated citizen groups (Tea Parties, "Birthers", environmentalists, and others) made up of citizens who are frustrated, angry, uninformed/misinformed, and gullible, to form and act in ways that reinforce behavior of the conspirators at the expense of their own ultimate self-interest.

The tone and content of public discourse is taking our country to the edge of a deep, dark abyss. Politicians are initiating a process of fear that generates anger (two sides of same coin) and evokes tones of cynicism, sarcasm and hostility. Behavior of most people is currently based on emotion with notable absence of logic reason and use of intellect. Media is ready to escalate fear and anger as a proven source of ratings increase.

Politicians and media are encouraged to promote emotionally based behavior because those who are emotionally driven are easily manipulated. All in all, nature of public discourse is likely the greatest threat to creating a desirable future for our country.

A fundamental principle of discipline is; "Order in any organization (government, business, community, family) is achieved only through self-discipline. Externally applied discipline does not create sustainable order, but only administers punishment to those who lack self-discipline, in baseless hope they will reform their behavior."

REFLECTIVE PROCESS FOR RESPONSIBLE CITIZENS

<u>Citizen</u> is a member of a nation who owes allegiance to it by birth or naturalization and is entitled to full civil rights.

<u>Responsible</u> behavior takes a stand on core values that serve that which is right and good and seeks to share influence with others who are like minded while aiming to influence others to redirect their actions and behavior.

<u>Reflective process</u> means to plan and execute a path of constructive action and evaluate learning and understanding of the processes required for success in achieving a greater good.

Those of us who are enablers of unconsciously incompetent, unconscionable, and unconscientiously based behavior in the corporate-government arena, may have our own version of these issues. In order to be a viable force in resolving destructive behavior in the corporate-government arena we ought to take an objective look at our thinking and behavior and decide what we need to learn about and change in ourselves. An objective view includes evaluating behaviors and actions that have made a contribution as well as those that have come up short or failed the test of doing what's right.

1.   Examine the level of consciousness I employ in response to statements from corporate executives, politicians, media and citizen groups:

>   -Am I sufficiently informed on the subject to adopt a thoughtful, values based point of view?

>   -To what extent am I motivated to only act out of emotional response to messages from these sources?

>   -What actions will I take to become able to respond from a fact based, reasoned position that reflects my core values?

2.   Examine my behavior in terms of conscientiously doing my duty as a responsible citizen of the United States of America.

-Cite examples where I have/have not behaved as a responsible citizen.

-As I become aware of the factual truths behind corporate executives and politicians positions, statements and actions, what is my position in response to them and what actions will I take in an attempt to call them to account for their behavior?

-What strategy (including alliances with like minded citizens) might I employ to produce effective action?

3. Examine aspects of conscience that direct my behavior as a citizen.

-Where have I been asleep to the reality of what is happening? What is the consequence of ignorance to me and fellow citizens? What is my feeling about this state?

-Where have I been aware of what is happening but did not know how to deal with it? What is the consequence of failing to prepare myself to take competent action? What is my feeling about this state?

-When have I known what to do but held back for fear of creating upsets or making waves? What is the consequence of failing to do what I know needs to be done? What is my feeling about this state?

4. Summarize what I have learned from steps 1-3.

-What of my experience has made a contribution and needs to be built on? What experience is in the form of baggage that is holding me back and I need to let go of? Where do I lack needed experience?

-Based on what I have learned from my experience, what steps do I need to take to become capable of doing my duty as a citizen?

-What does an examination of my feelings in step 3 tell me what I need to do to manage the expression of emotions such that they energize behavior that I want to express vs. that which is counterproductive?

-By calling on the best of my experience and properly directing emotions, what specific actions am I prepared to take as a responsible citizen? What will I do to gain experience that I lack? Who might I work with in the course of developing myself and taking planned actions? How will I and they audit our actions to maintain our course and correct it when it deviates from plan?

CHAPTER IV

CAVEAT EMPTOR: BUYER BEWARE

EXTRACTING VALUE FROM CUSTOMERS AND

OTHER STAKEHOLDERS

CHAPTER V

SUSTAINABILITY: AN EXERCISE OF INSUFFICIENCY

ORGANIZATION DESIGN AND SUSTAINABILITY

The aim of this chapter is to call to the attention of key leaders a distinct possibility that their organization will be unable to sustain its present course as well as any future course they decide to take, that this issue may be largely due to the fact that their organization exists not by design but by accident, and that there are proven actions they can take to reconcile this issue.

Subjects to be addressed include;

- Limited concept of sustainability

- Current state of organization design

- Current practices in organization design

- Suggested approach to reconciling issues of design

Operational definition of terms:

- Sustainability: "Capability to preserve access to the necessities of life and continuing acquisition of that which gives endurance, support, and strength." Organizations are currently using this concept with a generally external focus, as in products that contribute to sustainability of the physical environment. While this is a worthwhile commitment, it is an empty promise and an exercise in short-lived PR if the organization itself is not sustainable.

- Design: "A methodology for producing blueprints, specifications, and constructive approaches for the creation of viable wholes." Designing begins with the whole in mind, including purposes that justify its existence and core process that are the source of vitality necessary to sustain organization life and enable fulfillment of its purposes. Designing employs known, proven techniques in a deliberate, patterned, and managed process that specifies dimension and functions of internal parts critical to effectiveness of the whole, how they are to constructively interact, and their contribution to success of the whole.

- Organization design: "Applies the methodology of design to the members of an enterprise and the work that they do on its behalf. It includes structuring of their work within the structuring of the organization itself, processes that define actions/behavior/thinking that are at the core of organization effectiveness, and systems that enable higher levels of work effectiveness and continuous improvement."

- Development: "Involves distinctive change from practice of existing design, through redesign and aims to achieve higher levels of individual and organizational capability, state, and purposes."

- Leadership: "A systemic approach that influences active involvement of organization members in the process of designing the organization within which they have a part to play, and in committing to live out that design in their everyday work." Leadership is in contrast to supervision, a non-systemic approach that tells people what they need to do, how they should do it, and how they are to be.

Current state of organization design:

- Precise use of the term "organization design", understanding its significance, and employment of its techniques is virtually unknown in today's organizations. Accurately stated, organizations have come into being by a process of accident, response to randomly diverse and mostly external influences, acceptance of directives from those in authority and ultimately a reflection of unconscious incompetence in the arena of organization design.

- Current practice of organization design would be by analogy, similar to designing a chemical process by; choosing a couple of reactors, some pumps, a heat exchanger, a bunch of tanks, connecting them with available piping and operating the whole with an enticing, off the shelf controls package. Output would be whatever it was. *(Even moderately successful organizations are deliberate and disciplined in design of products and technology.)*

- In the absence of coherent designs, development becomes impractical, in that parts are not integrated in support of one another and in their contribution to the whole. Therefore the investment in changing an individual part runs the risk of further separating it from other parts and the whole. For example the mad dash toward "World Class Manufacturing" and "Baldridge Awards" has been largely unproductive and at times counter-productive.

- In the absence of design, organizations lack those definable and respectable qualities of character and integrity that are fundamental to sustainability in the face of;
  -pervasive rundown effect of entropy (demographic loss of key skills)
  -reduced ability to reconcile threats from the external environment (stock price, oil price, credit crunch)
  -revolt, abandonment, demise of key stakeholders (collapse of US textile industry, cooking the books)
  -competitive demands that require maximum realization of product and technological potential

Current practices in "organization design"

By example, the following illustrate the non-systemic, piecemeal approach that has led to the present state of existence of virtually all of today's organizations;

- Job design and pay levels by Hay
- Information management by SAP
- Manufacturing best practices by McKinsey
- Quality control by ISO
- Business strategies by BCG
- Organization effectiveness by latest CEO best seller
- Cost reduction by 6-Sigma Academy
- Performance appraisal by Jack Welch
- Engineering by myriad of sources
- Manufacturing operations by low cost contractor
- Personnel systems by Towers-Perrin
- Change management by Andersen Consulting/Accenture
- Safety by Self
- New thinking by way of imported senior management
- Training and Development by books and consultants favored and imposed by anyone in authority

These illustrate tendency toward a patchwork approach to forming an organization from a broad array of sources each of which aims to determine what the organization is and what it does. *These sources* operate from widely ranging and some times conflicting values, are focused on *their* own goals, use methods and approaches that *they* are comfortable with, and often take more knowledge with *them* than they leave. Much of the value that is available from these sources is lost because the organization lacks a sense of whole and inter-connected parts for them to interact with, and their effect tends to increase boundaries between internal units. And often times, these sources are perceived to be bringing the latest program du jour which are not by definition, sustainable.

<u>Suggested approach to reconciling issues of design</u>

- Any organization that can define itself as a potentially viable whole has the possibility of:

- Engaging influential hierarchical figures and key leaders in a process of understanding and grasping the value of organization design and establishing strategic direction for a design effort, and

41   *Ken Wessel*

- Contracting for guidance from sources of proven expertise and practical experience across a range of design situations, and starting the process by
- Outlining the scope of design work; organization whole, its core purpose and core processes, and then

- Charter, organize and initiate the design effort using values based principles of the organization to guide the effort.

CHAPTER V

SUSTAINABILITY: AN EXERCISE OF INSUFFICIENCY

ORGANIZATION DESIGN AND SUSTAINABILITY

CHAPTER VI

SETTING THE STAGE FOR SELF-DESTRUCTION

CONSEQUENCE OF UNCONSCIOUSLY IMPULSIVE ACTION

For purposes of this chapter we define impulse as; "a sudden inclination to act in response to some form of resistance, threat or adversity." Self-destruct means to harm oneself as a result of inherent flaws. Reference to organization indicates that these impulses are located in the organization itself vs. its products or technologies. Therefore the title of this paper refers to "An organizations rapid response to perceived threat that activates internal flaws in such a way as to harm the organization itself." The ultimate flaw is absence of a conscientious response to threat that aims to preserve long term health and viability of the organization and to endure short term discomfort and upset.

In today's business reality, resistance/threat has many sources:

- Stakeholders (customers, owners, suppliers, society, employees) who either withdraw some measure of their investment in the enterprise or at best hold at current levels.

- Decline in credit and other sources of financing

- Increasing demands for investing in "green" operations and products

- Uncontrollable impact of global influence via markets, trade policy, exchange rates, political ambition, shortage of natural resources, climatic upsets, etc.

- Pervasive climate of pessimism and declining confidence among constituents

Signs of unconsciously impulsive behavior:

- "All hands on deck" obsessive focus on problem solving and problem containment

- Throwing some assets overboard and allowing others to wind down toward counter-productivity

- Abandonment of future oriented events and activities that produce change and improvement.

- Increasing emphasis on; supervising (at expense of leadership), centralization of authority, power and decision making, and imposition of restrictive rules, boundaries, and directives

- Withdrawal from position of influence, partnering, and active involvement in value chain direction and operation

- Responding to uncertainty by creating illusion of certainty

Following is further detail on inbuilt flaws that actualize self-destructive behavior:

Problem Solving and Problem Containment

Even in best of times people become absorbed in containing or solving problems, because;

- Plugging a leak or fixing the leak brings instant gratification.

- The itch to spring into action trumps the value for upfront thinking through the situation and forming most logical approach.

- They lack capability to act at higher levels, including eliminating source of problems by drawing on own experience to create higher standards, or to design new approaches.

- Their plate of "go-do's" is overflowing so they make a quick hit on current problem and move on.

- The organization rewards and recognizes perceived short term success, "fire-fighting."

This behavior is self-destructive because it consumes time, energy and resources in activities that by definition, do not improve the state of the organization, its performance, or results. If the culture is locked in habitual behavior at this level by its fixation on threat, the organization will expire when its reservoir of resources is depleted.

<u>Mismanagement of Assets</u>

Assets are elements of the business that act on materials such that materials are transformed from specified input values to output products of greater value that are able to meet stakeholder needs. Materials include base chemicals, products of nature (ore, crude oil, air, etc.), information, thoughts and more. Assets do not become part of the output and are not used up in the transformation process although they may wear out with extended use and lack of maintenance. Assets include equipment that manipulates material, people skills that enable proper management of equipment, and systems that increase effectiveness of people and equipment. Infrastructure, good will, reputation, employee stakeholders and support systems are assets that play a longer term role.

Assets may be acquired, developed, improved, maintained at status quo, allowed to run down or divested.

Structural flaws in thinking and resulting behavior that lead to asset mismanagement include;

- Financial accounting rules that classify people and systems as 100% expense which labels them as an item of cost that should be reduced or eliminated. If they were at least in part viewed as assets, cost associated with acquisition, development, and improvement would be treated as investment, subject to decisions based on rate of return.

- Failure to think through the contribution of skills and systems and establish metrics to track trends in asset performance in response to actions that span the range of acquisition to divestment. Hiring and firing of people is only measured in terms of personnel cost and perhaps quantity of work performed. Direct, credible cause and effect measurement of relationship between skill applied and results delivered is virtually non-existent.

- Willingness to sacrifice long term value of assets in order to produce short term financial blips by withdrawing maintenance and allowing them to decline in performance. It is paradoxical for management to mandate run-down of assets in order to reduce cost to induce a stock boost that favors shareholders when *at the same time assets that are property of shareholders are declining in value.*

- Automatic use of slogans like; "people are our most important asset," when in fact skills that employees willingly use to achieve essential business results are the real asset. Organizations do not understand that they do not own their employees, but that their employees own the asset value of their skills and ought to be regarded as empowered contractors.

Withdrawal of Support for Change and Improvement

This always fatal flaw is manifested by the belief that activities of change and improvement can be turned off in hard times and back on in good times as means to weather the storm without adverse effects. This flaw in thinking is rooted in failure to understand;

- Energy that fuels an organization flows from its culture. Cultures that value change and improvement are grounded in qualities of optimism, steadfast purpose, patience/urgency, calm, commitment to work for a better tomorrow, self-development, and making a sustainable difference.

- These qualities of culture enable a long term view and also produce better results in short-term work on problem solving.

- Cultures quickly recognize recurring patterns of bans on training, development and projects that produce change and improvement, as being based on automatic thinking

47   *Ken Wessel*

of management. Consequence is that the culture becomes grounded in qualities of pessimism, cynicism, hopelessness, self-doubt and acceptance of mediocrity with predictable loss of energy.

- Capability to work at levels of change and improvement require skills beyond those used in problem solving. These skills are not acquired, do not evolve and become rusty in organizations that wobble between short term and long term focus. In fact the net real focus is short term.

Supervision at Expense of Leadership

Supervision (the management of people) is favored when the focus is on short-term results and problem solving efforts. Flaws in thinking that produce this state;

- Illusion that supervision increases control in a situation when reality is that imposed control is limited to presence of the supervisor and acceptance of his/her authority. By depending on external sources of control (supervisor) people give up accountability for self-discipline which sets the stage for out of control situation at worse time . . . when supervisor is not equal to unusual, unexpected and threatening situations.

- Imposed rules, boundaries and directives relieve people of accountability to use their skills and initiative to improve performance and may in fact punish them for crossing the line. Therefore, the organization is deprived of access to higher order skills and flexible approaches to deal with dynamic forces.

- Leadership and change are inseparable. Therefore in a climate where supervision dominates and change is abandoned, those who have the will to lead, leave the organization, withdraw their support or worse, lead counterproductive efforts.

- Leadership is incorrectly treated as a matter of assignment, chain of command level, or position of authority, when in fact leadership is simply a demonstration of the process of leading.

Withdrawal From Active Involvement in Value Chain

It is common for organizations when threatened, to withdraw behind defined boundaries that separate them from suppliers, customers and others and to adopt a siege mentality. Flaws in this position;

- Suppliers, customers and other value chain players tend to lose vitality as a result and the entire value chain can become a burden that adds to initial threat issues.

- The organization may be abandoned as former partners look for more viable partners.

- Person to person and role to role relationships built up over time that facilitate the flow of value

- Opportunity for joint problem solving and/or business development projects are diminished at a time when they are of greatest benefit.

Creating An Illusion of Certainty

As internal and external performance indicators decline, management attempts to instill an air of certainty by issuing decisive directives that specify actions to be taken along with predicted improvement. But since this action is largely devoted to problem solving and containment, sustainable improvement will not occur. This initiates a new cycle of unacceptable results, more directives and so it goes. As these cycles repeat the organization develops a cynical attitude that the only certainty is that uncertainty about the future is here to stay. (Amazingly, some organizations have repeated this cycle at least annually for more than 15 years.)

Possible/Probable End States

As the organization itself is caught up in cycles of previously noted behavior it;

- Loses the will to persevere against "hopeless odds" and accepts mediocrity and endless struggle as the norm.

Ken Wessel

- Bottoms out at levels of performance capability limited to problem solving and problem containment.

- Experiences a dullness of spirit that is only aroused by extreme disaster or unexpected great, good fortune.

Even though prime producing technology may have been initially sustained at customary levels, organization behavior will cause it to decline in effectiveness. And products that have held their value for a time will lose their value edge as judged by customers vs. competition.

Finally the business will disappear as its products, technology and organization become value-draining vs. value-adding in its environment.

What to Do, Given Threat and Adversity as a Fact of Organization Life

Investment in leadership development is a proven approach that can prevent decline into self-destructive behavior or can reverse decline that is underway. An ongoing process of leadership development not only addresses each previously noted flaw in organization behavior but concurrently enhances the use of other methods for elevating response to threat. This is an investment that has a virtually infinite ROI.

Personal Reflection:

- Take note of individuals who seem to be firmly and authentically grounded in core values that they use as force of will to create visions of a better state of the organization. Engage them in dialogue in order to understand the mind set they use to step up to leadership challenges.

- Observe and take note of the approach these individuals take toward creating potential for change and their stand on working toward perfection. Engage them in dialogue to grasp their thinking as they lead change and aim for high ideals.

- Continue dialogue with focus on functional skills including; developing teamwork, project formation and leadership, designing roles, decision making, etc.

- Discuss with colleagues qualities that define how they engage with leaders in common effort to achieve goals, meet standards, generate improvement, etc.

- Summarize your observations about what a leader is and does and use this learning as the basis for initiating an organization investment in leadership development.

CHAPTER VI

SETTING THE STAGE FOR SELF-DESTRUCTION

CONSEQUENCE OF UNCONSCIOUSLY IMPULSIVE ACTION

CHAPTER VII

COST REDUCTION MADNESS:

A TERMINAL ADDICTION OF MANAGEMENT

INTRODUCTION

Choice of words in the title signal the central theme of the material that follows, therefore they are given operational definition so that writer and reader begin in tune with the same line of thinking.

Cost includes units of financial measurement accounted for by organizations; raw materials, operating expense, capital, supplies and assets of all kinds including skills that people willingly use to support the business.

Reduction means to lessen the amount of any targeted cost item . . . paradoxically, "at all costs!" Excluded are concepts of invest more wisely, control more reliably, achieve higher level of stewardship and manage more effectively.

Madness is a state of foolish, reckless and frantic behavior induced by fear, greed, or egocentric desire.

Cause and effect of addiction are equally involved with this state of madness. It is difficult to know the extent to which cost reduction provokes madness or madness leads to cost reduction. It is a catch 22 of colossal proportions.

Management has degrees of meaning. In a structural sense management are those who populate the organizations chain of command, primarily those at the top who wield greatest influence by authority. But management also includes the process of managing the affairs and tasks of the organization at all levels, classes, and functions.

Ken Wessel

<u>Terminal</u> is treated as absolute, in that nothing good comes of the madness of cost reduction, not even in the form of lessons learned or useful experience gained. It is as if events and activities of cost reduction are swallowed by some pervasive black hole.

MOTIVES AND MOTIVATION OF CORPORATE OFFICIALS

Sources of motivation that cause corporate officials to arbitrarily mandate cost reduction campaigns (motivation refers to internal energy sources that influence thinking, actions and behavior.)

- <u>Greed</u> in the form of lust for material gain especially money.

- <u>Fear</u> of exposing self image to demeaning external criticism and negative imagination that conjures up different forms of failure.

- <u>Arrogance</u> in the form of excessive self-pride and contempt for others.

- <u>Suppressed conscience</u> that allows for rationalizing harm done to stakeholders and future of the corporation.

- <u>Herd instinct</u> that takes note of similar behavior by other corporate officials, including books and business articles that praise this sort of behavior.

Motives have to do with the end states that Corporate Officials aim to create for themselves.

- Accumulation of stock options based on increasing share price that Wall Street encourages when corporation take an aggressive approach to cost and head count reduction.

- Creating a self-image of turn-around specialist, profit generator and hard nosed executive that plays well on Wall Street, with head hunters and in executive circles.

- To reaffirm power and control over individuals and the organization . . . no matter what.

SYMPTOMS OF TERMINAL ADDICTION

- A corporation who had no history of mandated head-count and cost reduction, in initial attempt to impose these controls inspired an EVP to declare; "I have 1200 people I can cut . . . can anyone top that?
- Site managers/leaders were required to sign 100% of buying requisitions, seriously disrupting normal flow of site work, diverting them from overall site direction and strategic work and a decided loss of credibility within their organization.
- Vice-presidents were deputized to approve all travel requests, leaving many customers with problems that received no attention, and sales/marketing efforts that simply withered.
- Imposed reductions in training, development and equipment maintenance (favorites for cost cutters) caused a reduction in productivity that effectively neutralized the impact of cost cutting and head-count reductions. Expense account manipulation masked the true effect.
- Cancelling investment in product and technology upgrade, advancing skill level of employees and creating a more spirited, responsive and dedicated organization directly mortgaged the future.
- Arbitrary decisions about who was to be terminated often left functional units with a void of critical skills and disrupted partnerships that made important contributions to the business.

LONG TERM AND OFTEN IRREVERSIBLE EFFECTS

- Loss of credibility of key leaders and chain of command figures such that their ability to lead and manage have left their organizations rudderless and wandering aimlessly.
- Arbitrary and imposed directives without support of logic, reason or open communication leaves the culture in a state of hopelessness, resignation and devoid of initiative to improve the situation.
- Most capable individuals who have credentials to join other organizations are in line for bail-out.
- Acceleration of the law of entropy results in need for a huge investment of resources to effect a turn-around. If resources are insufficient the net result is slow death or rescue by external forces.

Ken Wessel

PERSONAL REFLECTION

1. Reflect on your experience with mandated, directive requirements that imposed cost reduction and head count reduction rules and goals on the organization.

2. What particular effects have you observed?

3. What impact did these effects have on functional excellence, individual and process improvement and contribution to business results?

4. Do you associate with like minded individuals who could network to develop a logical and reasoned option to mandated head count and cost reduction?

5. What steps could you and they take to initiate a changed approach to resolve immediate financial issues that would leave the organization stronger, more healthy and better prepared for the future?

CHAPTER VII

COST REDUCTION MADNESS:

A TERMINAL ADDICTION OF MANAGEMENT

CHAPTER VIII

DIVERSITY PROGRAMS:

EXERCISE OF IRONY

It is common for corporations to claim to embrace diversity and to create a programmed approach to support those claims. These programs are highly structured, predictable and firmly in the control of corporate officials and consultants they hire to deliver the message. Their aim is often an exercise in cynicism that creates a gap between what they say they value in direct contradiction to fundamental and universal values and ironically often produces:

- Creation of a superficially positive external image that is the source of public awards, fuel for recruiting efforts and a veneer of respectability.

- Elements that satisfy letter of the law regarding equal rights at expense of doing "what's right."

- A gesture to minority groups that their interests are being considered; while force of authority creates boundaries that negate real interests of minorities.

- Classified groups that are defined by law as protected minorities but does not include diversity of style, ways of thinking, educational background, different experiences, and the ultimate uniqueness that defines the individuality of each person.

Examples of corporate programs include:

A large corporation celebrates Martin Luther King Day with an expansive, extensive celebration that features speeches by African-American celebrities and highly placed corporate officials. The celebration is day long and includes mirror celebrations at local sites with video links to corporate activities. Awards of various kinds are extended in recognition of contributions by African-American employees and pledges are made to support further efforts. Corporate officials say that this level of recognition is intended to represent valuing for all minorities, but other minorities take this as corporate doublespeak and find it to be somewhat insulting.

A large and critical manufacturing site created an internal African-American network. The effect of their action stimulated other minorities to demand their own networks and soon there were networks for Asian—Americans, disabled persons, Hispanic-Americans, women, and returning veterans. There were hollow claims that these networks contributed to business results, but they were in fact, self-serving and dedicated to advancing own class interests. The net effect was that network activities built walls between various classes, created competition for site resources and promoted a site culture that failed to find value or advantage in diversity. Prior to the blooming of minority networks the site was served by an organization development network that included a highly diversified membership and was valued by the entire site as a source of increasing involvement in business pursuits, personnel development and evolution of a healthy culture. As minority networks came into being they drew members from the Organization Development Network until it shut down for lack of active members and site support.

A fundamental issue is extensive use of consulting organizations who gain entry through appeal to corporate officials and operate under banner of their authority and form minority groups who are indoctrinated into consultants program.

Consultants typically promote their own philosophy and use programming techniques to draw local minorities into their belief system. The ultimate aim of many consulting organizations is to build local dependency on their presence and process.

Another critical gap is created by the difference between what we say we value and depth of conceptual understanding of the meaning of diversity. Lack of understanding gives rise to use of undefined slogans such as valuing difference that is the subject for the following poem.

Ken Wessel

ON DIVERSITY . . . YOU AND I . . . DIFFERENT . . . UNIQUE (Ken Wessel 1/1/2000)

We are different . . . you and I.
Of that we can be sure. It is
a truth.

How ought we regard that truth? Shall
we value the difference that exists?
"NO NEVER" I say.

Why do I say this?
It is because we cannot know the truth of how we are different.
I scarcely know myself.
I must not pretend to know you.

Our attention goes to what we value,
and if I value our differences, I forget to notice
who I am, and to simply accept you as a
singularly unique being. I fail to see my
own becoming, and that you are becoming too.

What then should we look for in each other?
It is the search for the true self within me.
It is accepting the unique being that is you.
It is supporting each other in our journey of becoming.

When we accept each other this way, and
when we engage in a common work we
bring diversity to life naturally, in our living.

WE do not need to create diversity in our lives.
GREAT NATURE has done that for us.
It is a truth of our existence.
Diversity takes care of itself.

I am not the same today as yesterday.
I will be different still tomorrow.
This is true for you as well.

The quality of our diversity constantly changes.
We cannot give it a name.
We can only let it be.

Those corporate officials who have commanded a programmatic approach that features lack of understanding the meaning of diversity have generated outcomes that include:

- The illusion of social benefit.

- Intense identification within a minority class that has caused objective self-criticism to become taboo, therefore restraining capacity for self-improvement.

- Level of emotional energy that launched minority networks and has ebbed, leaving many of them in a meaningless mode of automatically going through the motions of their diversity programming.

- Resources consumed have consistently exceeded value generated, guaranteeing that diversity programs will continue to be in the grip of the law of entropy.

- Attachment of negative emotion to "discrimination" (depriving others of their rights) when in fact discrimination is a neutral term used in choosing between options and also applies to unfair rewards that aim to seduce people to a state where they can be manipulated by rewards.

- Diversity training imposed by those in authority to settle lawsuits or unfavorable publicity tends to evoke resentment of minority groups.

- Intensive pursuit of evidence to support preformed positions at expense of seeking and reflecting on personal experience as means to understand talent, qualities and uniqueness of others. (Diversity is not a values issue . . . it is a fact of life that no one can change. Life would not exist without diversity. Each person is a unique individual, different in many ways from others and

Ken Wessel

with potential to use their uniqueness constructively when it is valued.)

- Creating a corporate atmosphere that objectively thoughtful people experience as wrong if not actually evil and others sub-consciously find to be at odds with their feelings about the right way to do things. (A persons "rights" are always subordinate to "what's right.") The issue with demanding my rights is when it is at the expense of needs and welfare of others. For example our "Bill of Rights" is actually a statement of what's right in that it is expected to be equally extended to all citizens.

Some organizations have resisted the temptation to edict a programmed approach to diversity, have accepted that it is a fact of life and have gained the benefit of leading the evolution of a culture that is grounded in natural value for taking advantage of diversity in all endeavors.

As a personal approach to understanding diversity we reflect on the following by looking within ourselves.

- Give examples of actively seeking to understand those who are different from me and intrinsically unique. How do I react to realizing the uniqueness of another person? Am I more likely to be drawn to those similar to me or to those who are manifestly different?

- What is my experience of discriminating between that which appears to be right and good and that which appears to be harmful and potentially evil? How able am I to conduct an open-minded search for evidence before passing judgment? What is my experience of changing position in light of new evidence?

- What are my beliefs regarding, "all of creation exists for a purpose and has potential to add value by virtue of its uniqueness," and "embracing sameness as a way of life leads to weakness?"

CHAPTER VIII

DIVERSITY PROGRAMS

EXERCISE OF IRONY

CHAPTER IX

EMPOWERMENT HOAX

SEDUCTION, COERCION, DELUSION OF CONTROL

Self-empowerment is addressed in section two, chapter XV, The Way Forward. Chapter IX deals with lapses of consciousness and conscience that lead to disempowerment and the consequence of those actions.

Disempowerment is a technique employed by individuals with hierarchical, expert or charismatic authority that they use in an attempt to command and control the actions, behavior and state of others.

A warning bell ought to ring every time we hear the voice of authority say; "I/we have empowered specific individuals or organization units to do _____." These statements are the nucleus of the hoax because those in authority only grant temporary access to their power and retain authority to revoke it; therefore others are not actually empowered, but dependent on authority figures for a temporary taste of what empowerment might feel like. The concept of delegation a popular management tool for disguised controlling of others, has become a cultural norm for widespread disempowerment.

BELIEFS THAT GENERATE DISEMPOWERING BEHAVIORS

- Those who practice disempowerment are grounded in a value system that is based on following beliefs:

- Those who are subordinate to me for any reason, are not to be trusted to follow their initiative or create own direction because they might damage themselves, others or the organization. The ultimate truth is "they might damage me in some way." Therefore they must yield to my direction and follow my orders.

- Those who are subordinate to me cannot be trusted to apply self-discipline, therefore they must obey rules that I have created, imposed and enforced. Rule-breaking leads to punishment and imposition of rules that are more strict and harsh.

- Those who are subordinate to me cannot be trusted to refrain from blaming others when things go badly or demanding special rewards when things go well. Therefore coercive and seductive practices are applied to manipulate their behavior toward a passive level.

Coercive practices include:

- Public exposure of errors, failure, poor judgment, etc.

- Threatened with-holding of favorable ratings, promotions, and salary increases.

- Negative entries to personnel file.

- Using corporate grapevine to cast a dark cloud over an individual competence and behavior.

Seductive practices include:

- Employee of the month awards; reserved parking spaces,

- Use of trips for training as a reward.

- Programmed pats on the back, thank you gimmicks, etc.

- Promised pay raises, promotions, etc.

- Granting of plum assignments.

- Public accolades.

Ken Wessel

CONSEQUENCE OF EMPOWERMENT HOAX

Consequence of disempowerment directly opposes a quest for empowerment; "it is our nature as human beings to pursue a course in life of our own choosing, in harmony with the environment we live in consistent with our sense of a personal destiny."

- Reduced self-esteem including dependency on authority for direction in task performance and often in establishing the course of one's life.

- Inflated ego with personal conviction that when things go wrong it is the fault of others and when things go well, I deserve a special reward.

- Cynicism and distrust of others (especially those in authority) who fail to behave in ways that conform to my needs and expectations. Authority may be feared even when it is not credible.

- Loss of self-respect by abandoning core values in attempts to curry favor from others or in fearful bending to will of others.

- Rejection of commonly held and shared values, principles, ideals and standards.

- Seduction into working for rewards vs. achievement of worthwhile results, can lead to self-loathing dependency on those who control the rewards.

- Covert behaviors and actions that include retirement on the job, sabotage, and fostering revolution as revenge for sacrificing self-control for control by others.

- Promises and the word of a disempowered person are discounted, therefore requiring backup plans, contingencies and replacement by others who are favored by those in authority.

IMPACT OF DISEMPOWERMENT ON BUSINESS CULTURES

- Organization members withdraw commitment to work for benefit of stakeholders in order to apply energy and resources to self-protection.
- Innovation, creative thinking and change initiatives are abandoned in order to avoid criticism, and direct denial of these efforts by those in authority.
- Individuals circle the wagons in an effort to mount a collective defense against continuing disempowering tactics of those in power leading to isolation from organization members and stakeholders.
- Those who are disempowered do not directly challenge those who are the source of disempowering tactics, and often band together to subtly undermine organization efforts to achieve operational excellence and business superiority.
- External organizations and individuals are frustrated in efforts to create working partnerships with organization members who are fearful of entering into agreements with outsiders.

PERSONAL REFLECTION

An objectively accurate view of our behavior is the first step on the road to self-empowerment; knowing ourselves is a fundamental requirement.

1. When have I served myself at the expense of others by bending to the will of authority? What core value was compromised?

2. When have others discounted my capability to deliver on promises or commitments? What core value was compromised?

3. When have attempts to take control of the course of my life failed? What core value was compromised?

4. If I were to take a stand on living by core values, what price might I have to pay? How would I and others benefit by taking a stand? What initial steps in that direction seem doable?

Ken Wessel

CHAPTER IX

EMPOWERMENT HOAX:

SEDUCTION, COERCION, DELUSION OF CONTROL

CHAPTER X

JOB DESCRIPTIONS: PACT WITH THE DEVIL

This chapter will compare and contrast job descriptions with role designs, beginning with an operational definition for each.

Job descriptions are standardized directions that outline tasks to be performed, specific duties to be acted on, and details of an employment position and activities that are the basis for payment. Job descriptions are written in conformance with a highly structured, rigid template and presented to potential job holders on a take it or leave it basis. Job descriptions are usually in the domain of HR function and are an integral element of culture that tends to be authoritarian, directive, linear and activity oriented.

Role designs are developed systemically involving input from potential role player and those who are affected by, rely on and support the role. These designs describe the proper part a person is expected to play interactively with other roles in common effort. Candidates for a role are expected to engage role design in order to understand what is expected and decide to accept/reject the role on basis of own judgment of ability to perform it satisfactorily. Role designs are elements of culture that tends to be empowering, purposeful, results oriented, grounded in partnership and developmental.

Purposes are not stated for *job descriptions* which promotes an inward focus on completing specified tasks, doing ones duty, with expectation of reward for living up to letter of job description,

Role designs are centered on purposes that justify existence of the role and reminds role player that he/she is serving a need greater than the role itself. The organization and role player are obligated to discontinue roles for which purpose no longer exists and to continually work to expand role to serve greater purposes.

Ken Wessel

Results are not specified in *job descriptions* and expectation is that performer will complete assigned tasks satisfactorily, and in effect "get the work done."

Role designs specify results the role performer is accountable to deliver to serve needs of those who depend on products of the work performed. Simply doing the work is not acceptable if desired results are not delivered. Therefore role designs provide a high value basis for calling a person to account for performance excellence. In addition, results specify principles that are to guide work performance so that effect of role players activities reinforce efforts of other role players and set the stage for continuous improvement.

Responsibility in the case of *job descriptions* is directed to those with authority to assign and audit work or to revise the job description. It is the duty of job performer to follow dictates of the job description and those who administer it.

Role designs call for role performer to engage in a spirit of responsive partnership, those who depend on results, those who provide resources required to produce results and those who are affected by role performance.

Authority refers to degree of command the job performer has over personal skills and state, resources, materials, and other means required to deliver results although in the case of *job descriptions* the issue is command of means to get the work done. This is the element of job descriptions that set up the job performer in a no win situation (pact with the devil) where specified performance is demanded without input or control over means required to deliver what is expected. In most situations a person is assigned to a job without opportunity to create a doable relationship between means and ends.

Job designs require balance between command of means and results accountability. Role performer is expected to assess whether command of skills, state, resources, materials, organization support, etc. are capable of producing results for which he/she is accountable. If doubt exists it is up to role performer and others involved to create a situation where results are in a doable range. Results expectations may be scaled back or command of means may be increased, or both.

Execution refers to activities and events that take place as job or role is performed. *Job descriptions* are almost entirely based on a list of activities and events that can be explicitly assigned and easily audited for completion. Elements of purpose, results, responsibility and authority are generally overlooked as a result of approaching the job with linear and habitual thinking.

Role designs make an explicit connection between use of means and execution of events and activities.

Role performer and those with shared responsibility are charged with using means to accomplish tasks that produce results effectively and efficiently without waste.

SYSTEMIC NATURE OF ROLE DESIGN

Role designs are systemic in nature with links between elements that are used to create balance, flexibility, and a natural process of growing the role and developing the role performer.

All elements are linked to role purpose in order to insure that the role performs to support purpose vs. serve self interest of role performer.

Authority is linked to results in order to insure that promised results are likely to be delivered. When authority is not up to results demands, performer and organization pay a high price in terms of failure to live up to responsibility, and performance issues that involve investment in problem solving efforts.

Responsibility is linked to authority in order to involve sources of means in a process of insuring that necessary means are available and are being used effectively and efficiently and that further investment of means is considered as route to expanding role and developing role performer.

Responsibility is linked to execution in order to provide for real time audit and feedback process based on partnership between role performer and those to whom he/she is responsible. Role designs treat auditing as a constructive process to keep activities and events on track and to work on continuous improvement of effectiveness and efficiency of events, activities and use of means. (Audits of performers constrained by job descriptions tend to demand conformance to letter of assigned tasks and look for punishment or corrective action when variance is noted.)

Execution is linked to results by standards and goals in order to insure that events and activities are on track to deliver promised results. Standards are used to achieve and upgrade qualities of performance, goals are used to insure that increments of progress toward results are on track. Effect of goals and standards provides an objective basis for auditing execution and measuring trends of growing the role and developing role performer. (An aspect of pact with the devil for performers limited by job descriptions is lack of objective measures of performance, while being judged subjectively in absence of specific agreed to goals and standards.)

SUMMARY COMPARISON OF ROLE DESIGN AND JOB DESCRIPTIONS

Job descriptions have these effects on task performers:

- Focus is on getting the work done in a way that satisfies supervisors.

- Task performers do not see the value of their work and cannot appreciate their contribution.

- They are evaluated by subjective measures without meaningful involvement in the process.

- Way out is to move up to a higher paying job and/or one that is less onerous.

- Are ultimately performing in a box that is created and maintained by external forces.

- Do not have naturally structured basis for partnering across boundaries.

Role designs have these effects on role players:

- Role can be approached each day with a sense of purpose.

- Results are visible in terms of contribution to others who benefit from their value.

- Each role is based on partnering with others in support of and contribution to a greater whole.

- Evaluations and progression are based on objective measures with role player in the process.

- Role has inbuilt energy and means for growing role and developing role player.

SELF-REFLECTION

The following self-reflection process is intended to activate would-be stakeholders who operate from bleachers or sidelines into those who decide whether and what their stake ought to be in organizations with whom they have a nominal relationship and are willing and able to design and perform a role that aims to influence organizational behavior in a positive and constructive direction.

An option for personal decision is whether to withdraw invested stake from a hopeless situation and re-invest it in one that has potential for achieving a sustainable contribution. Read and study chapters in Part B, "The way forward" for additional thoughts ideas about constructive stakeholding.

1. Review previous material and sketch model of job description and framework for role design.

2. Take note of and record your work experience in terms of relating to job descriptions and/or framework for role design.

3. Reflect on attitude toward previous experience in terms of everyday feeling of approaching

"A day's work and sense of accomplishment when day is done."
Summarize what has been learned from own experience.

4. Apply what you have learned to an action plan to engage your organization in a process of designing/redesigning the role you play. Outline for redesign follows:

    • Role purpose: "To become an active stakeholder in _____ organization with intent to bring constructive influence to its performance, contribution to all stakeholders and public behavior."

    • Accountability for results that include; "specific contribution to stakeholders that achieve metrics of _____ for each stakeholder, _____ principles that state your values with regard to corporate behavior, _____ method for providing feedback to corporations regarding your observations of behavior and performance."

    • Responsibility that you aim to share with specific organization members and expect to call to account for outcomes including: "—who have promised specific results to stakeholders, _____ who control effective use of resources and _____ who influence impact of corporate behavior on others across shared boundaries."

    • Catalog your authority over means necessary to achieve accountability and responsibility, including: _____ personal skills, _____ ability to manage own state and thought processes, _____ networks and partnerships you can call on for support, _____ ability to manage own time and energy, _____ other means you believe necessary to fulfill role design.

    • List events and activities you expect to engage in to execute your role as an influential and responsible stakeholder, including upfront work to achieve required authority.

5. When your role is redesigned engage those with whom you share responsibility in constructive engagement with their roles as well.

CHAPTER X

JOB DESCRIPTIONS: PACT WITH THE DEVIL

Ken Wessel

CHAPTER XI

WHERE HAVE ALL THE LEADERS GONE?
Where have all the leaders gone?
Betrayed by authority most everyone
placed in a box
just pounding rocks
hopes for the future all but gone.

This chapter will examine the impact of corporations (including media and politicians) that lack consciousness, conscience and conscientiousness for attributes of leadership:

- Four attributes that develop will to lead
- Four attributes that increase level of leader's functional skill
- Four attributes that define a leader's presence

WILL TO LEAD

Leadership will not occur without development of will within a potential leader that causes him or her to step forward and freely express elements of will to engage challenges that require able leadership to achieve success. Qualities of will include:

- **Focus** so that the leaders force is not diminished through diffusion or misused by application to wrong things.

- **Intensity** so that the effect of leading is felt to high degree and that its source can be known. The old axiom that leadership ought to be invisible is counterproductive and in fact an oxymoron. Leadership in order to be available to people and trusted by them, must be known in terms of who is the leader and what is the process of leading.

- **Tenacity** so that the effects of leadership are sustainable through time and that the leaders process is steadfast and does not waver in any circumstance.

Four attributes that develop will to lead:

- **Authenticity:** A leader's behavior is anchored in deeply held faithfully portrayed values to which they hold true in any situation.

    Corporate officials and others with authoritarian power unrestrained by conscience, commonly coerce, seduce, and manipulate leaders to rationalize abandonment of core values on a situational basis; "failure to conform will cause removal from a position of influence." This ought to set off alarms and call for an accounting of the behavioral shift that leads to wobbly direction and loss of credibility and offers of support to get leader back on track.

- **Vision:** Leaders operate toward a compelling vision of more desirable states for themselves, others and organization which becomes the north-star for their actions and continuously reinforces his/her motives and motivation.

    Corporate officials and others who are in the game for short term gains, fear risk associated with pursuit of vision and have a cynical and unconscious view of the future that cause visions to grow dim or disappear which ought to cause others to pause in their pursuits while they strive to re-establish leadership visions. Charging ahead without vision is effort without focus or meaning and steady decline of motivation. Visions must be factual so that others believe in them, work for achievement of vision, and partner with others. Vision is never dreamlike of a fantasy; but must be factual in terms of the life we aim to lead.

- **Change:** A leader welcomes and embraces change as the only logical course toward fulfilling vision and achieving everyday expression of values.

Corporate officials and others who are fearful of leader's natural process take the organization into unknown regions and take steps to discredit change as loss of control and unacceptably risky. Principle that leaders and change are inseparable will cause leaders in the face of prohibitions regarding change, to leave, withdraw or discover other avenues of change that often subvert organization norms. Consequence of failure to change is aimless wandering while the world passes by.

- **Ideals:** Pursuit of ideals serve the leader, others and organization as high road of thinking and behavior through an ingrained commitment to work for perfection of self, organization, technology and products.

Corporate officials, politicians and media are possessed by cynicism that tells them perfection is unattainable, requires up-front investment, faith in what is possible and they therefore lack will to mount a conscientious effort to achieve more than "what is good enough." Giving up pursuit of ideals ought to be a source of personal (and national) shame or embarrassment and lead to energized effort to restore wounded pride. Life without ideals is a meaningless experience of mediocrity.

Able managing of will in the real time dynamics of a leadership process depends on conscious, thorough preparation so there is a reference point to manage against.

Frame-works serve this purpose, by calling attention to variances and their consequence as they occur, so leader can call on self and others for corrective action.

INCREASING LEADER'S FUNCTIONAL SKILL

Exercise of will without sufficient skill often leads to chaos, unproductive or counter-productive outcomes, and loss of faith and trust in leader's process. Unfortunately many so-called leadership training and development programs focus on increasing knowledge of technique at the expense of understanding what they mean, how they are best used and that application must be influenced by exercise of will. Further discredit is brought to concept of leadership by automatic reference to those high in chain of command, politicians and experts as "leaders" while many/most of them lack any discernable leadership capability.

Four attributes are involved in increasing leader's functional skill and promoting successful thinking and action:

- **Ground for successful functioning** is built largely on a nucleus of strong, individual partnerships that become the genesis of teamwork. This ground becomes a rallying point for organizing and directing action as well as a reliable source of positive, constructive energy.

  Unfortunately corporate officials have been overcome by a concept of "team-building" and import consulting organizations that employ gimmicks, unrealistic exercises and emotional appeal to create a façade of teamwork without investment in developing the real thing. Wise leaders understand that teamwork is guided by different principles than team-building; and that the nucleus of creating teamwork is generated by partnerships that support the team.

- **Goals for successful functioning** are focused on creating viable value chains (including our organization, origin of natural sources of materials and ultimate recycle/reuse) own internal value adding processes and consciously accurate mapping transformation of inputs into outputs of greater value. These goals apply to processing of materials, thoughts, information, etc; and products are directed to serve the needs of stakeholders in the organization.

  Unfortunately corporate officials have looked inward at promoting own success, often at expense of the value chain, therefore putting an entire industry at risk and often pursue a course of acquisition and divestiture as short term means to economic viability at expense of playing a clearly defined role in value chain operations and development. All too often stakeholders are taken for granted ("they need us more that we need them") and are named as stakeholders vs. being created through a process of stake-holding.

Ken Wessel

Wise leaders understand that control of inputs to our value adding process, support of assets, and maintaining a healthy environment are all at discretion of stakeholders.

- **Direction for functioning** is largely determined by design of roles and role relationships. When roles are united by partnerships and teamwork and exist to serve stakeholders through value chains and value adding processes they become a powerful force for establishing, maintaining and upgrading direction that the organization follows. They have the stabilizing and course correcting qualities of a gyroscope that maintains direction no matter the impact of external conditions.

  Unfortunately corporate officials are dedicated to job descriptions that maintain a narrow focus on tasks to be performed, duties to be fulfilled, and audit of how well the job is performed without focus on results that serve stakeholder needs and sustain a viable value chain. Underlying values are for worker control, simplicity, basis for reward/punishment, and a supervisory process. Wise leaders understand that effectiveness in playing a well designed role is the key to success of all other roles and of the whole.

- **Instruments that support effective functioning include:**
  -Critical event mapping that identifies each event in logical sequence that is required to achieve significant objectives, establishes accountability for event success and established resource requirement for a successful effort.
  -Decision making as a systemic process that integrates elements of force, energy, information, mechanics of deciding on action, position, or judgment and consequence of actions taken.
  -Making change happen as next logical step once potential for change to occur has been established as an act of leaders will in a way that achieves the highest level of possible outcome.
  -Meeting design and leadership to cause all meetings to generate a high ROI on investment of time, energy, and resources while stimulating people to become involved in promoting successful meetings and avoiding those that are wasteful.

Unfortunately corporate officials are drawn to latest fads, books by other corporate officials and pronouncements by business school academics in deciding what functions to support at expense of investing in systemic, internally developed and organic processes.

Wise leaders understand that these functions are best performed in an atmosphere of teamwork, are critical to success of sustaining viable value chains, and are to be appropriately incorporated into all roles.

DEFINING A LEADER'S PRESENCE

A leader in order to become effective must have an identity, be visible, known to others and ideally unified with other leaders. Attributes that define presence:

- **Grounding is in high priority value for self-empowerment** beginning with leader's capacity for self-management of will, function and state in any circumstance. When leader masters own level of empowerment, next step is to create an empowering environment for others.

  Unfortunately corporate officials are intimidated by empowered subordinates and resort to a process of delegating own authority which they call empowering others, even though it is obvious to all that authority can be with-drawn at discretion of supervisor. Wise leaders understand that no one can empower another and can contribute to an empowering experience and that a culture of self-managed individuals will out-perform a culture that is passive by nature.

- **Goal of a leader's presence is to establish living systems** that are sustainable through time, self generating, consume minimum energy and resources, manages boundaries that invite partnering, is dedicated to continuous growth and development, and is committed to serving others.

Unfortunately corporate officials shy away from systems that enjoy this degree of self-sustaining interdependence and dedication to serve a greater good and prefer to establish external boundaries within which they can control behavior and actions. Wise leaders understand that living systems partner with other systems in symbiotic and synergistic processes so that each of them and their stakeholders are assured of continuing benefit.

- **Systems establish and maintain direction that reflect leader's presence** in a way that is focused on achieving critical results, motivating for participants, stimulates continuous upgrade and employs efficient mechanics. Systems integrate structures and processes and create organizations rhythm.

Unfortunately corporate officials lack foresight and investment mindset to see value in designing and sustaining up to date systems and often allow outdated systems to drag down organizations performance. Wise leaders understand that predictable and sustainable, effective and efficient performance is largely based on well designed systems operated by empowered individuals in support of living systems. Intelligent systems create rituals that build self-discipline and successful habits. Systems become the gyroscope that maintains direction of the organization, in times of storms and adversity.

- **Leaders through their presence enforce two taboos;** waste in any form is wrong, corrective action is required and failure to observe and manage own behavior is not tolerated and again, corrective action is required.

Unfortunately corporate officials are often the initiating force for waste as a consequence of self serving and self indulgent behavior. Self observation of behavior and openness to corrective action is foreign to those who believe they have arrived at a level where behavior and actions are beyond question. Wise leaders understand that a taboo regarding waste builds spirit of conserving that which is essential, builds pride and self-disciplined behavior and is often a critical factor in becoming dominant organization in an industry. And that observing own behavior is the most direct route to self-empowerment, relieves others of need for frequent evaluations and corrective action plans, and is the source of true pride in own development and achievement.

SELF REFLECTION

Scan the entire chapter, choose subjects that are energizing and draft a statement that defines where you and your organization currently operate in terms of leader's will, function and presence.

1. Draft a corresponding statement that illustrates characteristics of leader performance that would move the entire organization to dramatically higher levels of purpose, function, state, performance and competitive position.

2. Identify behaviors of authority figures who initiatite issues that restrain closing the gap.

3. Choose several issues and outline actions you could take as a leader partnering with other leaders to resolve issues and allow for closing the gap.

4. How likely are you to act?

CHAPTER XI

WHERE HAVE ALL THE LEADERS GONE?

CHAPTER XII

SELF-SERVING MOTIVES:
WASTE WITHOUT REMORSE

I have personally witnessed many of the following events and activities or have first hand accounts of others from reliable sources.

- I was invited to lunch by two VP's of a corporation that was in danger of losing most important customer. Lunch lasted three hours, involved two bottles of expensive wine and cost in excess of $120. (My two employers P & G and SaraLee had an inflexible rule against consuming alcohol during working hours so I excused myself.) I understood that the lunch was reimbursable as a business expense, which meant it would be deducted as cost of doing business and that the VP's would be late for scheduled meetings. When I raised concerns about this behavior the response was the usual RHIP, "rank hath its privileges." I avoided all future invitations to lunch and became involved with mid-level directors in designing and leading productive meetings.

- A large corporation used a designated corporate jet to ferry employees from HQ to major sites for meetings, task team work, etc. At the last minute on numerous occasions corporate officials would commandeer the jet for own travel causing employees to cancel meetings, work sessions and in general create a waste of time, planning, and opportunity for value adding work.

- Corporate officials in many corporations routinely use administrative assistants to shop for and purchase gifts for family members and friends. Time involved becomes a deductible business expense.

- Revenues, shipments and expenses are often shifted across monthly, quarterly, and annual time boundaries in order to

Ken Wessel

place financial results in most positive light to impress Wall Street and inflate bonus payments. Result is that management of financial matters defies analysis, trends are no longer valid and employees lose motivation to do their best to achieve best possible stewardship of financial affairs. These behaviors may fall short of Enron type manipulation, but are covered by same sort of motives.

- Arbitrary reductions in force are also calculated to impress Wall Street and drive up stock price and bonus payments. Net effect is that investment in developing career level expertise, internal and external working partnerships, savvy that comes with years of experience is wasted without opportunity for continuing ROI. Impact on culture, confusion regarding roles and role relationships represent waste that is never calculated in net impact of reduction in wage expense.

- Arbitrary imposition of spending rules includes requirements that Site Managers (no matter the significance of their site) personally approve ALL purchase orders, VP's approve ALL travel requests, sourcing professionals decline purchases that violate short term guidelines, etc. Net effect is that strategic work is abandoned when it is at highest priority, individuals in chain of command feel disempowered and are viewed in that light, capital improvements that have winning ROI are abandoned and in general the organization withdraws significant support for achieving promised product values. Again, reasons for these edicts are to impress Wall Street and inflate bonus payments. Culture takes on a siege mentality and begins to circle the wagons in defensive mode including withdrawal of initiative to invest in change and continuous improvement.

- Office locations and furnishing are a primary status symbol among corporate officials with competition (often involving dirty tactics) to upgrade office furnishings and office location to indicate higher status. Upgrades include art work, antique décor, built-in bars, spacious surroundings, and other fashion touches intended to impress others. The net effect is waste of corporate resources, time and potential of those involved and general disrespect by employees for the behavior they observe.

- Most corporations and governmental agencies have strict rules against accepting gifts and certain kinds of entertainment. If the level of innovative thinking that is used to circumvent these rules were applied to business interests, business results would take a steep upturn.

- A variety of actions are taken by corporate officials that have the effect of mortgaging the future by focusing on short term interests, results and gains. It is likely that those responsible are conscious of the long term impact, they however ease their conscience with rationales that if I don't do it, I will be replaced by someone who will be worse, an undeniably hollow, self-serving argument. These actions include:

-Elimination of training and development activities that in effect cause a negative trend in applied use of the most important asset of any organization; "skill, effort and capability of employees willingly contributed to benefit the business."
-Cancellation and/or reduction in capital investments that aimed to deliver more productive and business effective products, technology and organization.
-Assignment of able leaders to mundane fire fighting and routine tasks eliminates change and continuous improvement efforts and causes leaders to withdraw from active leadership, leave the organization or to work against it.

WHAT IS WASTED AND CONSEQUENCE?

- The list of what is wasted (based on previous examples) is nearly infinite and includes; expense $'s, value adding time, sound basis for intelligent business decisions, talent, potential for improvement, depth of experience, credibility, integrity, investment in more competitive products, technology and organization capability.
- Waste of any kind is a high level taboo for any healthy culture and is supported by high priority values of members of the

culture. Evidence of waste initiated by corporate officials is cultural poison.

- When corporate officials are personally wasteful of organizations assets and materials, organization members are tempted to play the same game with attitude, "what's the value of expending effort to prevent waste when it goes unrewarded and unrecognized."

- All classes of stakeholders will soon recognize wasteful habits at expense of confidence the organization will continue to provide them products and services that meet their value needs and cause them to look for other sources.

- Other stakeholders operating on principles of integrity will tend to disconnect from organizations where waste is not only tolerated but initiated by corporate officials as a matter of course.

PERSONAL REFLECTION

- Reflect on the course of your life as a whole and take note of what you have learned regarding values and practices that aimed to limit waste.

- How well have these values served you and your organizations over the years?

- What issues have you encountered that tended to resist your efforts to prevent waste?

- State what actions you and others have taken to resolve those issues.

- Identify actions you and your colleagues are able to take to reduce sources and levels of waste in your present organization and others where you have a stake.

CHAPTER XII

SELF-SERVING MOTIVES: WASTE WITHOUT

REMORSE

CHAPTER XIII

THE WAY FORWARD: LEADERSHIP DEVELOPMENT: KEY TO A DESIRABLE FUTURE

Following is a prospectus on "The Leadership Development Forum" a seminar series on leadership development that has been presented to more than 1800 participants, in 35 seminar series, 7 countries and with a 100% success rate. Participating organizations include; DuPont, Conoco, Procter & Gamble, GE, Honeywell, FMC, Vulcan, Fiberweb, James River, Englehard, OCI and others. Included are principles that guide LDF and a leadership assessment process to determine subjects that need work to elevate level of leader effectiveness.

THE LEADERSHIP DEVELOPMENT FORUM AN OFFERING BY KEN WESSEL

The Leadership Development Forum (LDF) is an offering that participants attend as members of natural work groups and collectively challenge their leadership ability to deal with significant real world subjects in realistic time frames. Participants in LDF develop an action orientation toward leading a team based pursuit of opportunity and resolution of issues with a sense of urgency and authority.

PURPOSE OF LDF

To learn, develop, share and practice leadership skills in a way that;
- Applies to everyday work (will be recognized by others as a practical approach)
- Extends beyond best known practice of leadership (other offerings focus on "how to" advice and fail to draw from experience of participants as the most valuable source of learning)
- Focuses on current leadership issues (vs. dissection of case studies)

- Expresses culture, values and needs unique to our organization (enables folks "back at" to quickly tune in to a more effective leadership presence)
- Brings added spirit and cohesiveness to our team

So that the organization is able to develop from within, those qualities of leadership needed to generate continuous, healthy growth of the business, its people and its stakeholders.

PARTICIPANTS CAN EXPECT TO GAIN CAPABILITY

- To come to understand ones own values and to rely on them as foundation and compass for behavior, such that it is perceived by others to be genuine, reliable and energizing.

- To stimulate others to believe in their vision of a better future and commit to work hard for it

- To approach the unknown with courage, confidence, curiosity and expectation of discovery.

- To prepare for change by building potential for it to occur.

- To take a visible stand for ideals of behavior and performance as the high road to excellence.

- To maintain a healthy balance of patience and urgency in stepping up to what must be done.

- To understand the nature and significance of hope in oneself, others and organizations, and how

- To personally appreciate the power and value of teamwork and to grasp the qualities and behaviors involved in creating it.

- To acquire deeply felt respect for the value chain and dedicate our role in it to serve stakeholder needs as critical success factors for business and individuals.

- To observe ones behavior objectively in real time and to use personal experience as primary means for self-development.

- To think in a more orderly, disciplined and focused manner especially when under pressure.

- To grasp what is required to behave as an empowered person with capability to maintain an appropriate personal state in any circumstance.

These capabilities are not to be taken as a checklist, formula or imitation of leadership by others. They are part of a whole to be worked on and applied interactively and always subject to improvement. It is not expected that these will be totally new skills, but rather that participants will build on skill they already have, learn from their experience and gain new insights that enable them to become more confident, complete, capable and thorough in their practice of leadership. The essence of LDF goes beyond increasing *knowledge* about leadership to *understanding* the nature of leadership, what it is, the way it works, what it can achieve and how it is developed. Understanding is developed by learning from experience via designed exercises within LDF sessions and involvement in designed action plans between sessions. Learning is validated by reflecting on the effect of applied leadership to real world opportunities and issues.

PREMISES ABOUT LEADERSHIP

These premises are statements of belief, based on experience with leaders and leadership. They are offered for study, testing and modification to use as a basis for further thinking about the subject, and are foundation thinking for LDF design.

- THE AIM OF A PERSON WHEN LEADING IS TO BE AN INFLUENCE IN THE LIVES OF OTHERS, BUT THEY DISCOURAGE OTHERS FROM USING THEM AS ROLE MODELS.

- LEADERSHIP DOES NOT OCCUR AS THE RESULT OF ASSIGNMENT, ROLE, LEVEL, CERTIFICATION, OR SENIORITY

- LEADERSHIP, CHANGE, AND DEVELOPMENT ARE INSEPARABLE. AN ORGANIZATION WILL NOT SURVIVE IN THE ABSENCE OF CHANGE; THEREFORE LEADERSHIP IS CRITICAL TO SURVIVAL OF THE ORGANIZATION.

- A LEADER IS GROUNDED IN REALITY, WORKING TO PERFECT IT <u>AND</u> ORIENTED TOWARD THE FUTURE, WORKING TO CREATE IT.

- LEADERS GAIN RESPECT BECAUSE OF THE VALUES ON WHICH THEY TAKE A STAND AND RISK THE LOSS OF RESPECT WHEN THEY BECOME IDENTIFIED WITH WHAT THEY OPPOSE.

- EFFECTIVE LEADERS INFLUENCE OTHERS BY STIMULATING THEIR THINKING AND CAREFULLY AVOID EMOTIONAL APPEAL AS AN ENERGIZING TACTIC.

- LEADERS ARE GROUNDED IN PERSONAL EMPOWERMENT AND CREATE AN EMPOWERING ENVIRONMENT FOR OTHERS. THEY UNDERSTAND HOWEVER, THAT THEY CANNOT EMPOWER ANOTHER PERSON.

- A LEADER IS CONSCIOUSLY AWARE OF THE CONTENT OF OWN THOUGHTS, IS ABLE TO VISUALIZE THEIR TRAJECTORY THROUGH TIME AND SPACE AND ESTABLISHES A COMMUNICATIONS MEDIUM THAT INVITES OTHERS TO JOIN HIS/HER PROCESS.

- PEOPLE ARE NOT ABLE TO ADOPT THE LEADERS VISION, BUT RATHER NEED TO BELIEVE THAT LEADER HOLDS FAST TO A VISION THAT PROJECTS A DESIRABLE FUTURE FOR THEM AND THE ORGANIZATION. WISE LEADERS INVOLVE OTHERS IN DEVELOPING THEIR OWN PERSONAL VISION CONSISTENT WITH LEADERS DIRECTION.

- PEOPLE DO NOT ACTUALLY "FOLLOW A LEADER." RATHER THEY FOLLOW THEIR OWN LEADING THOUGHTS THAT MAY HAVE BEEN STIMULATED BY THE LEADERS PROCESS.

PEOPLE GAIN STRENGTH AND FREEDOM IN PRESENCE OF ABLE LEADERS BUT DO NOT BECOME "LEADER DEPENDENT."

- THE BEST WAY TO GET A "FEEL" FOR THE EFFECTS OF LEADERSHIP IS TO OBSERVE ONES OWN RESPONSE TO A LEADERS INFLUENCE.

- THE CULTURE OF AN ORGANIZATION WILL GO ONLY AS FAR OR DEEP AS A LEADER WILL TAKE IT.

- A CREDIBLE LEADER IS EFFECTIVE AT MANAGING HIS/HER OWN STATE, EVERYDAY AFFAIRS, AND ONE OR MORE FUNCTIONS VITAL TO THE ORGANIZATIONS PERFORMANCE.

- FRAMEWORKS ENABLE HIGHER QUALITY OF THINKING BY STIMULATING ORIGINAL, USEFUL, WHOLE THOUGHTS AND FACILITATING ACCURATE, CONSTRUCTIVE EXCHANGE OF THINKING AMONG INDIVIDUALS.

FORUM FORMAT

- Structured as 3-4 natural work groups of 6-10 members. Previous groups have included VP-GM teams, site staffs, task teams, networks, new product/site design teams, etc.

- Basic Forum structure is 5 two day sessions at 4-5 week intervals. Structure has been modified to accommodate needs of particular Forum groups.

- Each group chooses a subject (current, significant issue or opportunity) as the focal point of their work in forum sessions, between sessions and beyond.

- Sessions conclude with a segment for group planning to apply learning to their selected issue between sessions. Next session begins with group reports on how plans worked out, what was learned, and questions they have.

- Materials, concepts and frameworks are introduced and discussed in general forum setting and applied to selected issue by individual groups in designed exercises. Groups report their experience for general forum discussion.

- Each group selects one or two members to work with Ken Wessel in advance of each session to develop capability as process resource to their group during and between sessions.

LDF HISTORY

The Leadership Development Forum is copyrighted by Ken Wessel and was originally designed for
DuPont where it was delivered more than 20 times over a period of 12 years to 1000+ managers, professionals, executives and key non-exempt leaders.
LDF has been delivered to a number of organizations in the US and six other countries.
It is common for participating groups to maintain a networking relationship in order to share learning experience that advances real world leadership capability.

SAMPLING OF PARTICIPANT REFLECTIONS

VPGM of a global business; "Our development in LDF as leaders and as a business team enabled a positive transition that created ongoing synergy as we merged with _____."

Managers of sister sites; "Our leadership teams formulated major site change strategy during LDF, and implemented it soon after. We have improved performance of both sites by sharing resources, creating best practices, and continuing to network on leadership development."

Newly assigned HR Director; "It was here at LDF that I found the courage I would need; not in anything I learned to <u>do</u> but rather in leaning what kind of person-what kind of leader-I really needed to become.
In answering the question; 'can I do this?' I <u>knew</u> that a great deal of preparation had gone into the program and I <u>knew</u> that Ken Wessel, our

forum leader was a skilled and trusted professional." (A few years later she was appointed to an important director role in the Clinton Whitehouse.)

Corporate Engineering Staff; "We used our LDF leadership team development experience to actually increase energy, focus and performance as we transitioned from sudden loss of our manager to health issues to assignment of a temporary replacement and on-boarding of a new manager."

Manufacturing and HR VP's; "Our work at LDF as members of senior staff led to a major overhaul of the
HR approach to manufacturing and creation of a stronger link to the business. Two key site managers and their staffs (including HR professionals) will attend next LDF to further develop the new approach."

New business design team; "We're getting a better sense of ourselves as a team and the culture we aim to create. We need to figure out how to transfer this learning to others as they come on board and to internalize in the organization the skills that Ken brings."

PRINCIPLES THAT GUIDE THE LEADERSHIP DEVELOPMENT FORUM

The following principles are used as guides to insure that The Leadership Development Forum lives up to beliefs that are expressed in premises about leadership that will be engaged in the first session.

- Effective leadership depends on understanding what leaders are and what they do. What a leader **is able to do** defines level of effectiveness and sets stage for positive qualities of a leader to emerge.

- In order for a person to develop they must lead the process. Skilled and experienced resources may provide useful guidance and coaching but must never relieve a person of accountability to lead own process.

- Understanding anything requires learning from own experience by reflecting on previous experience or learning from conscious involvement in new experience.

- Learning from peers, trust in own experience and reducing teacher dependency are elements of a learning process that promotes understanding. Conversely, intensive pursuit of knowledge via leadership training is insufficient and can be a barrier to understanding.

- Task leadership of team exercises and between session action plans and documentation of learning experience are inbuilt LDF processes.

- Pace of LDF will be managed to allow for understanding to develop.

- Effective leading is never a "lone wolf" process, and is exponentially increased in impact when partnered with like minded individuals focused on high priority work.

- Leadership development is an open-ended process to be supported by internal resources (who will be involved in own development as part of LDF.)

STATE OF LEADERSHIP ASSESSMENT PROCESS

Following is a guide for assessment of state of leadership our organization with process steps:
- Individually, indicate on scale where you see current practice.
- Each person place rating on flip chart prepared to include all ratings.
- Discuss meaning of pattern of rating.
- Individually, indicate on scale where you believe practice of leadership needs to be to achieve operational excellence and business effectiveness.
- Place ratings on flip chart and discuss meaning of patterns.

- Discuss significance of the gap and identify subjects for work that can close the gap. These will be subjects for work in The Leadership Development Forum.

LEADERSHIP AND ORGANIZATION HEALTH

STATUS QUO/ HEALTHY GROWING
STAGNATION BUSINESS SYSTEM

Clarity of Direction
Individuals and groups follow the course is clear to all a path determined by external x—x—x—x—x—x—x—x through clear and timely forces or by self-interest communication of leaders strategic thinking

Teamwork
People compete for resources teamwork is encouraged and rewards, at the expense of x—x—x—x—x—x—x—x by demonstrated leader others, if necessary values for sharing, mutual support and cooperation

Action/Results
Action is provoked by external energy and enthusiasm
Administration of rewards x—x—x—x—x—x—x—x are evoked by progress, with the leader, toward objectives

Risk Taking
People are either unaware of Leaders understand that risk and are victims of it, or pursuit of opportunity fear risk and withhold best x—x—x—x—x—x—x—x involves risk and take effort action to reduce it

Vision
Work is experienced and Leader builds motivation seen as a linear sequence of x—x—x—x—x—x—x—x toward work by helping tasks assigned by others people see value in the results

Integrity
People obey rules and policy Shared values with leader in proportion to the force of x—x—x—x—x—x—x—x and others is basis for external authority constant support of principles and standards

Communication

Communication is controlled Leader engages others in by authority and features one—open direct dialogue with way processes of telling x—x—x—x—x—x—x—x belief that differing views are a source of strength

Standards and Expectations

Standards are used to sort The leader and others aim out superstars and failures to pursue high standards and to administer rewards x—x—x—x—x—x—x—x that lead them to mastery and remedial action in their profession

Development

Energy, skill, and resources Leader develops people are used up in pursuit of x—x—x—x—x—x—x—x toward potential at a rate short term goals and faster than it is used up fire fighting daily problems

Empowerment

Decision making is highly Leaders create an bounded with limits set by empowering environment level, title, certification, x—x—x—x—x—x—x—x through encouragement, and other artificial challenge and support of designations decision making by those most qualified

Coaching

Training and coaching are Leaders treat coaching and treated as techniques for x—x—x—x—x—x—x—x training as an investment in cost control, rewarding improving capability, and morale building performance and conribution

Performance Management

Organization initiatives Leaders use organization are treated as extra work initiatives as material for and implemented with a x—x—x—x—x—x—x—x setting direction, focusing, minimum of effort and and improving commitment

Customer Focus

Customer demands and Customer success is used by feedback are used to x—x—x—x—x—x—x—x leaders as a visible symbol apply pressure for of organization excellence better results

Trust and Mutual Respect

Intensity of rules and Leaders are predisposed to policy creation and x—x—x—x—x—x—x—x extend trust and respect to enforcement presumes others without pre-condition people are not trustworthy that it must be earned

CHAPTER XIII

THE WAY FORWARD

LEADERSHIP DEVELOPMENT:

KEY TO A DESIRABLE FUTURE

Ken Wessel

CHAPTER XIV

THE WAY FORWARD:
CONSCIOUSLY DESIGNED ORGANIZATIONS

CHAPTER XIV PURPOSE

To bring a new and useful perspective to the subject of organization design and development in a way that generates interest in continuing research, study and application, so that we are able to use our organizational roles as means to upgrade design, and promote an increasing rate of healthy growth.

OPERATIONAL DEFINITIONS

- <u>ORGANIZATION</u> refers to people, materials, resources and assets that come together to create products of value sufficient to achieve stated purposes and stakeholder needs and to the managing of technologies required to generate those products. Organization is the element of an enterprise that integrates with product and technology to maximize everyday effectiveness and efficiency while continuously building new potential.

- <u>DESIGN</u> is a patterned and managed process that employs known and proven techniques to produce the most viable answer to questions of "what, why, how, who, when, and where" concerning the structuring and function of someone or something. Design methodology produces blueprints, specifications, and constructive approaches for creation of viable wholes. Designing begins with the whole in mind, including purposes that justify its existence and value adding processes that are the source of vitality necessary to sustain organization life and fulfill its purposes. Designing specifies dimension and functions of internal parts critical to effectiveness of the whole, how they are to constructively interact and contribute to success of the whole.

- <u>ORGANIZATION DESIGN</u> applies design methodology to members of the enterprise, the work they do on its behalf and provides them tools and techniques to manage energy in all forms (human, material, financial, natural.) It includes structuring of the organization itself, processes that specify and define behaviors, actions, and thinking that determine organization effectiveness and systems that enable higher levels of work effectiveness, continuous improvement and change.

Design also includes organization philosophy as a core values driver, the energizing effect of value adding work, guidance by commonly held principles and actualizing concepts that define what the organization is and what it does.

- <u>DEVELOPMENT</u> is a process of raising the purposes, state and functioning of a person, organization, technology, or product to a distinctively higher level of intrinsic and extrinsic value. Development is a special aspect of change based on recognition of unused capacity that has value adding potential and an investment mindset that transforms untapped potential into increasing contribution that generates a positive ROI.

- <u>LEADERSHIP</u> is a systemic approach that stimulates active involvement of organization members in designing the organization within which they have a part to play and in committing to live out that design in everyday work. Supervision in contrast to leadership is a non-systemic approach that tells people what they should do, how they are to do it and the way they ought to be.

PREMISES ABOUT ORGANIZATION DESIGN

- Designs aim to create organizations that reflect conscious intent vs. an accidental happening.

- Virtually all organizations approach product and technology design with significantly greater levels of seriousness, attention and discipline than they apply to organization design.

- Organizations get by with a low level of investment in organization design because competition takes the same approach; therefore a level playing field.

- Change and development efforts lose their effectiveness in a poorly designed organization.

- Organization design/redesign depends on capable leadership and is a prime responsibility for leaders.

- Typical returns from long term investment in organization design, redesign, and development are orders of magnitude improvement in business results, employee capability and contribution, state of technology and sustainable healthy growth.

GROUNDING FOR ORGANIZATION DESIGN

Following are beliefs and principles that form the foundation and supply positive energy for design of an organization that is accountable to conscience and dedicated to conscientious effort to serve a greater good. These statements are taken from designs for several organizations that I have worked with, that have consistently served the needs of all stakeholders, are guided by dedication to do what's right and are committed to develop better products, technology, and organizations that are increasingly able to serve a greater good through time.

BELIEFS ABOUT PEOPLE

- People have a natural desire to grow and develop, and as evidence of their development, to influence and modify the world about them.

- People want to be part of a stable group of individuals who they respect, with whom they share a value adding purpose, and who provide constructive challenge and support toward one another.

- People want to have access to opportunities for development . . . . gaining and using new capabilities to increase their contribution.

- People are drawn toward accountable and responsible behavior, and able to be self-directed and self-disciplined.

- People enjoy applying imagination, ingenuity, and creativity to their work.

- People benefit and gain satisfaction from being part of a group that is able to openly express feelings and needs.

- People look for a manageable amount of challenge toward their own and team development and are energized by pursuit of higher achievements.

- People want the right to question what is going on and to participate in changing it if it needs changing, in order to develop a caring, effective and healthy system.

BELIEFS ABOUT DEVELOPMENTAL CULTURES

- A developmental culture supports the continuous and simultaneous evolution of individuals, organization, technology, and products.

- A developmental culture works on effectiveness before efficiency.

- A developmental culture gives people the opportunity to achieve dignity and meaning in their lives through value adding work.

- A developmental culture encourages people to use their own will, energy, and creativity to direct, design, and create value from work.

- In a developmental culture, the work itself provides the organizing form for people, their roles, and the work that they do, vs. levels, jobs, and functional stovepipes.

UNIVERSAL TRUTHS HELD BY
DEVELOPMENTAL ORGANIZATIONS

- It is RIGHT that people should look forward to coming to work.

- People WILL do their best without promise of reward.

- People PREFER to lead an orderly, disciplined life.

- Freedom CANNOT be granted.

- Cooperation and belonging are NATURAL human desires.

- People ASPIRE to serve others and improve their world as evidence of that effort.

- We value most what we have paid a PRICE for.

- Even though the world ought to be a better place, we cannot FORCE it to be so.

- People have an instinctive distaste for WASTE of themselves and their resources in idle and non-productive pursuits.

- We have a shared OBLIGATION to be our brothers/sisters keeper.

PRINCIPLES OF HEALTHY GROWING WORK CULTURES

- Each member is expected to do any work, for which they are qualified, in support of business needs.

- Teamwork is essential for a person to develop toward their full potential, and increases the contribution for which they can stand accountable.

- Each person is accountable for providing leadership in developing themselves and the work that they do.

- The vitality of a business is multiplied when the value-adding-process becomes the primary source of motivation for work and the development of people.

- The only source of a viable career lies within a healthy, growing business.

- A persons career path is marked by progressively building on blocks of skill that become an expanding base for value-adding contributions to the busines

- The asset value of a person is measured in terms of the skill (function-being-will) they acquire and successfully apply to business needs.

- Each person is expected to maintain an integrated relationship between;

    -their work
    -the value-adding-process
    -stakeholders needs and expectations
    -their personal development

These principles are especially useful in guiding the design of systems for personnel development.

PRINCIPLES FOR LIFE AND WORK IN A DEVELOPMENTAL COMMUNITY

- Life of the community is renewed through acceptance of one another. (The more conditions that we place on others, the more conditions that we place on ourselves, until we are so conditioned that development cannot take place.)

- Those who have must give and work for those who lack.

- The reward for a work effort may be in the form of a significant challenge or personal temptation; not including expectation that we ought to be thanked for our effort.

Ken Wessel

- Faith in natural patterns allows what needs to happen. (Trusting only in our calculated planning limits the potential for something new to develop.)
- Members of the community do not seek, nor have, power and authority over one another.

- Whatever you would have others do to you, that is what you should do to them.

MANAGING PROCESS PRINCIPLES

- EXERCISING ACCOUNTABILITY: People are to be depended on to do as they say and to pursue their own accountabilities, independent of expending effort to check up on others.

- INTERACTING: There must be a strong bias toward communicating in a face to face manner with an appetite for energetic engagement at a self:self level, usually in groups, and always aimed at developing something better.

- DIRECTING: Organization members are self-directing in that they establish and pursue their own course within the scope of direction they receive in regard to serving stakeholder needs.

- AUDITING: There is a rigorous and intense, ongoing process of comparing activity, behavior, and results to standards, ideals, principles, and targets, with the intent to continuously improve value adding work performance.

- DISCIPLINING: Each person, team, and organization unit must exercise the force of self-discipline, restrain behaviors that are taboo, and overcome the grip of personal likes and dislikes in order to pursue doing what's right and minimize the need for discipline from external sources.

- EMPOWERMENT: Each person accepts and acts from the potential that exists within them, to generate responsible behavior in pursuit of the right thing to do and in working for a greater good.

QUALITIES OF ADVANCED ORGANIZATION DESIGNS

- Maintains focus on purposes that are a central feature of an evergreen view of desired end states.

- Is energized, in part, by the challenge inherent in constantly renewing missions.

- Accepts "governance by principle," but does not take them for granted.

- Has and employs political savvy, but always in serving larger whole needs.

- Functions as an open system that values products from customer's point of view.

- Has an informal, dedicated group of influential thought leaders who are keepers of the philosophical base

- Has and expresses the experience of unity.

- Has visible leaders who instill hope as an ingredient of their leadership process.

- Accepts a state of tension as a natural element in a change oriented culture that is constantly striving toward perfection.

- Uses systemic and systematic ways of thinking as a conscious means to reverse the law of entropy.

CHAPTER XIV

THE WAY FORWARD

CONSCIOUSLY DESIGNED ORGANIZATIONS

CHAPTER XV

THE WAY FORWARD
SELF EMPOWERMENT: CHOOSING OUR COURSE IN LIFE

EMPOWERMENT: FREEDOM TO SERVE THE PURPOSE OF OUR EXISTENCE

The intent of this chapter is to stimulate thinking about the subject of empowerment. It is written from a perspective of empowerment as a natural pursuit for all human beings, as we aim for increasing authority, command, and control of our everyday affairs and the course of our lives. This is true of our life as a whole and extends to each domain of life and the roles that we play in them. The extent to which a person succeeds in this pursuit is measured in degrees of empowerment, which include contribution to a greater good, dependably doing the right thing, attracting others to join with them, and achieving a personal sense of satisfaction and fulfillment.

Terms of empowerment are three-fold;
- Extent to which a person is self-directed, meaning they have power to set their own course and reasonably expect to follow it, includes force of self-initiative a person is able to bring to any situation. Implication of this is individuals do not need to draw power from external authority as stimulus and source for their thinking and behavior.
- The extent to which individuals have power for self-discipline in any situation. This means they control their own behavior responsibly in accord with an agreed to "code of conduct," which includes principles, rules, guidelines, policy, law, etc., that apply to situations into which they have freely placed themselves. Self-discipline includes power of a person to freely choose self-denial and sacrifice when it is the right thing to do and serves a greater good.

- The extent to which individuals have power to be self-accountable for the consequence of their actions and behavior. This means they refrain from blaming and self-justification when things go badly, and from expectation of special reward and recognition when things go well. They are therefore free from control by external sources of coercion or seduction.

Implication of this concept of empowerment for those in authority, is profound. Authority as used here includes implied exercise of command and control of others by virtue of hierarchical (supervisory) position, being a source of special expertise (skill and knowledge needed and valued by others), and emotional dominance, (charisma, psychological stimulus). For those in power, the empowerment of others involves facing particular facts;

- I cannot empower another person, or ultimately dis-empower them, although there is much I can add to an environment that favors one or the other.
- Therefore, empowerment is not something to be granted, for if it could it might as easily be taken away, which places "empowering others" in the class of a charade. In fact, the only true source of power when empowering "them," is and remains, the authority figure.
- Delegation, a somewhat old-fashioned term was a concept of "I charge you to act on my behalf and within the specified scope of my authority which I extend to you for a defined circumstance." The more modern use of term "empowering others" has the same essential intent.
- A person responding to authority is ultimately accountable to follow directives of that authority and submit to its force. The subordinate is not truly accountable to give their best because of the controls placed on them by the external source, and therefore, the paradox, "I know they can do better, why don't they?" or "I know I can do better, why don't they let me?"
- A primary source of authority for those in supervisory positions (all levels of chain of command except the lowest) stems from their control of rewards, punishment, and information. These controls must give way to other forms of engagement if an empowering environment is to be created.

- An empowered person cannot be coerced or seduced by external authority to betray personal core values, self-image, or obligation to do the right thing.
- An atmosphere of dis-empowerment is pervasive in highly structured, authoritarian organizations and those in authority generally suffer most from issues of insufficient personal power. They are in a special bind created by desire to control their subordinates, while being limited by the controls imposed on them by their supervisors.
- So what needs to be considered for a process of individual empowerment to be effective?
- This must be treated as a complex issue with variables that are unique to each situation. Therefore the people involved, including those perceived to be in authority and those governed by it, must come together in an open process that seeks true empowerment for all.
- It is essential that those leading and guiding the process are operating from an empowered state and have a personal stake in others becoming empowered.
- The process requires those involved to come together on common ground of beliefs, philosophy, and principles regarding empowerment, which they have mutually developed. Their aim must include development and exercise of personal power as a source of increasing service to a greater good.
- It is critical that those involved, exercise increasing individual power in all its dimensions as it evolves, which includes a great deal of patience and faith in the process, in order to endure the inevitable setbacks as they occur.
- Self-empowerment is a fundamental requirement for exercise of effective leadership and obligates leaders to work for creation of an empowering environment for others.

In summary, it is the rightful state of human beings to grow in personal power, to use it wisely in doing that which is right and serves a greater good, and to support one another in this effort.

RESPONSIBLE EXERCISE OF FREEDOM

Common issues confronting the leadership nucleus of an organization are in the form of restraining forces from their environment, from external authority, and from within themselves. As they struggle to properly exercise leadership and honor personal core values, the organization risks becoming dispirited, reactive, and sliding toward instability. These issues are reconciled when leaders are able to objectively see themselves in the reality of their situation and others in similar situations partner with them in a process of shared learning. Following premises offer guidance in the process of resolving issues.

PREMISES

A primary effect of leadership is to free others in terms of their thinking and actions. This effect is caused by influence from a leader who is personally free in his or her thinking and likewise free to take what they believe to be proper actions. Becoming free in thought and action involves the coming together of three forces;

- Initially a reconciling force which involves accepting the reality (truth) of a situation and the consequence of own actions when a choice is made to alter it in some way. This applies to both internal (personal) and external (environmental) aspects of the situation. Once reconciled, a person is free to face up to and engage relevant issues.
- Restraining force exists in the form of issues that conspire to freeze the situation or cause it to deteriorate. (Again, this includes internal and external issues.) Leaders must be able to observe issues impartially, free from the grip of emotion. Those issues that control the situation must be openly declared and separated from faux issues that are simply noise in the system. When issues are thoughtfully engaged, a person is free to activate a response to them.
- Choice is now available to initiate an activating force that expresses personal core values, aims to resolve issues, is mindful of reality, and considers the range of possible consequences in taking actions.

Responsible use of authority requires those who exercise it to seek mutual influence with those who experience its effects. This includes three primary sources of authority;

- Authority grounded in chain of command position ought to be a source of wise direction setting.
- Authority grounded in expertise ought to be a source of learning by others that leads to increasing capability.
- Authority grounded in leadership ought to evoke motivation in others to seek and work for change and development of self and surrounding environment.

The real and true hope for the sustainable, desirable future of an organization and its members is that its leaders are themselves able to perform at increasingly higher levels of work and to take the organization with them. This provides evolutionary direction and motivation for the organization as they deal with issues of:

- Damage control and problem containment in order to survive (stabilize level work)
- Problem solving in order to get operations and behavior on standard (operate level work)
- Trusting and learning from experience in order to upgrade procedures, and working to achieve higher standards (advancing level work)
- Application of powers of creativity, innovation and organization resources to re-design of products, technology and the organization (improving level work)
- Creating whole new and viable forms of product, technology, and organization (regenerate level work)

Long term health and growth depends on leadership that performs at two levels beyond the organizations center of gravity."

INTERNALIZING PREMISES

Those who form the leadership nucleus of an organization have opportunity to test these premises by working to personalize and internalize forces that could free them to take the organization to levels more able to secure a desirable future for the business and its stakeholders. The process of testing premises involves application of individual values, experience and thinking to the situation at hand and openly sharing in the experience as it unfolds.

The first condition for becoming free is to be reconciled to:

- Transcending ego and self-interest as primary motives
- Taking an objective view of organizations in decline in terms of eroding business, organization and individual performance, steady decline of spirit, and shift of motivation from serving others to saving self.
- Accept the consequence of own actions
- This warning; "anyone who is not personally reconciled in this manner must not be included in the process and excused without blame or penalty."

Conclusion to be reached before proceeding is that a sufficiently internalized reconciling force frees a person to face the issues that define and control current state.

The next condition for becoming free is to be objectively open to issues that represent restraining force:

- Chain of command authority from corporate officials is grounded in desire to control others and is closed to engagement with others in any process of mutual influence. It lacks sufficient understanding of business organization core processes to establish viable direction.
- Those individuals who are most expert in operations lack authority to capitalize on their expertise due to devaluing of their function by chain of command and own willingness to accept a state of minimal credibility.
- The leadership nucleus and others who have previously demonstrated capability to lead are unable to extend this capability beyond organizations boundary/interface, at the expense of declining credibility among them and within their unit.
- Leaders time, energy, and attention is being absorbed in personal management of destabilizing forces (internal and external) that appear in the form of unsafe, hostile, cynical, apathetic, and self-centered behavior compounded by arbitrary, unexpected, random and counter-productive demands from the environment.

- Lack of experience and ethical guidance in planning and conducting engagements with chain of command authority.
- Warning that issues within leaders themselves must be faced up to and worked on as a prior condition for engaging issues that involve others.

Conclusion to be reached before proceeding is that stage is set to purposefully initiate generation of activating force.

The determining condition for becoming free to lead in this situation is to become a self-activated leadership nucleus that designs and executes an activating force that aims to resolve restraining force issues and honor reconciling force values.

- Individual values will have been exercised and increasingly visible as these forces emerge. They now need to be reflected on, clarified, and shared as common ground where leaders come together to take a stand (when necessary) and as a constant source of will and energy to initiate the effort and stay the course.
- Leaders need to create a collective vision of future state of the business, the organization and its members that they believe in and are willing to work for.
- A course of change needs to be mapped out in logical sequence, with milestone events (suggested elements follows.)
- A couple of ideals to be held up; "Desired change in others and/ or the environment is first tested and experienced by ourselves," "an able and experienced guide is in place as a condition for embarking on the journey," "the activating force is evolving, evergreen and inclusive of others as they are able to take on a role." "Once initiated, the course of events must play out to a logical conclusion, an abandoned effort will likely produce a worse situation than before."

COURSE OF CHANGE

Is grounded in principles:

- Initiate no action without a plan
- Pre-think possible consequence of action to extent practical and timely . . . then move on

- Keep the process moving (appropriate audit and reflection are forms of movement)
- Act in concert as a leadership nucleus
- Rescue a team member in trouble and challenge one who is lagging
- Identified sources of issues are not to be treated as the enemy, but rather to be engaged with expectation that they have capacity to become part of an activating force that resolves the issue
- Confidentiality may be appropriate, deception is not
- Do what is personally believed to be right but challenge that belief when it fails to serve a greater good
- Being open to sacrifice in pursuit of a greater good is necessary, however a person cannot sacrifice what is not theirs or they cannot live without

Is focused on purposeful goals

To achieve a dramatic shift in conduct of all aspects of the corporation, its businesses and individual members, in a way that;

- Immediately shuts down actions that are clearly harmful to any stakeholder
- Reinforces and invests in improving on actions that add value
- Initiates actions to fill voids defined by gap between current state and vision

So that influence generated by leaders causes all forms and sources of authority to coalesce as a single strong force in service to a commonly held, greater good."

Follows a predetermined course of events

- This suggested sequence should be outlined in full before launching with increasing detail added as time for events draws near. No event should be bypassed and needs to be satisfactorily completed before next event occurs.
- Define, clarify and share personal core values and guiding principles as common ground from which to lead the effort.
- Create vision that reflects mutual understanding of and commitment to work for the greater good to be served
- Test the current state of issues, set priority for engaging them, and identify the authority that is in primary control

- Paint a picture of what could be achieved if each primary source of authority could shift from current mode to one that is more responsible.
- Build a base of irrefutable logic to establish a position that functional expertise and site leaders will continue to contribute to the greater good of business pursuits.
- For each issue, state an objective to be pursued in resolving it, a process for engaging the controlling authority in the resolution process, time and place for the engagement, and roles to be played. Design and leadership of this meeting ought to expect it to be a transforming event (point of no return.)
- Provide for follow-up to each engagement so as to invest in taking advantage of new opportunities that develop.
- Audit and reflect on the process to this point, capitalize on learning, engage newly emerging issues, and plan next phase.

And has access to essential instruments

This includes capability of leaders to manage themselves in a high-stakes challenging process, available group process and meeting design skills, an able guide, accurate relevant facts, and command of the personal time and energy necessary to see the effort to completion.

Ken Wessel

CHAPTER XVI

THE WAY FORWARD
WILL TO BECOME ... TO DO ... TO BE

PREMISES ABOUT WILL

* It is the exercise of will that causes us to become more of our true self, to do that which is beyond previous capability and to be a continuously evolving, developing person.

* The future will occur. As it enters our present, patterns of force and energy determine conditions of our existence through the effects of fate which is exercise of external will.

* We can however generate and act from potential to influence the shape of our future; to build toward our expectations. This is related to living our destiny and requires exercise of will from within.

* Therefore, as we approach or aim to create turning points in our lives, career or business, it is necessary that we command the force of will required to take the path of our choosing.

* These premises apply to individuals and to organizations.

* Essential aspects of will are:

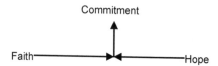

- Faith generates the aspect of will that causes us to move into new, unexplored territory; to pursue new challenges and dreams, to go beyond experience.

- Hope generates the aspect of will that causes us to stick with an effort through good times and bad and see it to completion.

- Commitment generates the aspect of will that causes us to fully invest our skills, our spirit, and our minds in the work/Work at hand.

PREMISES ABOUT FAITH

- Faith is the act of believing without proof or evidence. "The substance of things hoped for, the evidence of things not seen."

- (Trust conversely, is belief based on convincing experience or accepted body of evidence.)

- Faith does however seek validation through experience or evidence.

- Faith provides link from ideal/perfection to actual/practical.

- Faith is found in processes of change or creation and therefore has its place in real time action vs. reflection on experience.

- Oftentimes a person is unaware of their faith and simply becomes certain that what is to become, will become and what must be done, will be done.

Ken Wessel

TRIAD OF FAITH
Belief in what is to be created

Belief beyond Absence of
proof   certainty

What must be done

PREMISES ABOUT HOPE

- Hope is trusted fulfillment in form of a favorable outcome to an effort or endeavor.

- Hope is strengthened by adversity, withstands disappointment, and seeks no guarantee.

- Hope inspires a search for answers to questions for which there are no words.

- Hope is an essential quality to be found within all leaders.

- Hope is evoked by challenge found in opportunity and sacrifice involved in seizing it.

TRIAD OF HOPE
Understanding that what must be done
can be done

Accepting the

in and from what is personal
Recognition of worth

price to be paid

PREMISES ABOUT COMMITMENT

- Commitment is best thought of as part of a triad with Love and Compassion:

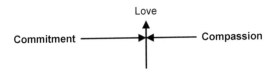

- Love, commitment and compassion have the common quality of being unconditioned and that each is completed and made whole by the other two. The implication of this relationship is that a separate and additional creative act is required to bring the reconciling aspect of will into existence.

- The special power of unconditioned reconciling will is apparent when we consider that faith may be strong, weak or blind; therefore subject to conditions. Hopes likewise may be high, faint or false.

- <u>Commitment</u> involves pledging or obligating oneself to a deliberately chosen course of action. This unforced choice creates a path that "opens a path." When truly committed to a line of work, the work takes over, a condition often referred to as "flow" or "being in the zone." Note that commitment to a person or to a goal is an inappropriate concept; one that involves surrender of will to external sources of influence.

- <u>Compassion</u> involves deep feeling of sharing the suffering of another, including desire to alleviate it and receptivity to the possibility that we cannot.

- <u>Love</u> involves consciously held, strong feelings of affection for others. It causes us to imbed deeply and resolutely in the mind, a caring considerate regard for the rights, feelings and good of others.

TRIAD OF COMMITMENT

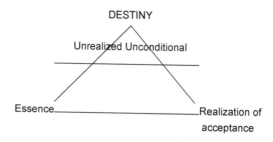

PAYING THE PRICE

Special note is taken of issues that arise to restrain an activating will even in the presence of a whole and viable reconciling will. These issues seem to center on receptivity to paying the price and include issues related to absence of certainty and unconditional acceptance. A fundamental, universal source of these issues is found in desire to hold on to what one has, coupled with unwillingness to let go of control. Therefore premises about "holding on-letting go" are offered for reflection and debate:

- Holding on stems in part from desire for control and certainty. At extreme it creates the opposite; being controlled by external forces and loss of control when exposed to a dramatically changing environment.

- An ancient philosophy; "the misery of uncertainty is more powerful than the certainty of misery."

- When vision is sufficiently strong and compelling, letting go of "what is" initiates a necessary and natural process of moving on. (Activating and reconciling aspects of will are able to produce their effect.)

- A central issue in developing and exercising will is deciding what to give up/let go of and what to acquire/take on.

The ordinary view of paying the price is expressed in slogans; "you get what you pay for," "no free lunch," "A view worth the climb," "no pain-no gain." What these phrases miss is the essential nature of real sacrifice as means for direct engagement with issues that restrain our will. Premises about sacrifice:

- Sacrifice is an unforced decision to let go of (surrender) something of personal value, to which we may be attached. it expect to be paid back in any way, (bargaining and deals are not part of sacrifice.)

- We cannot sacrifice that which we do not actually have or which has no meaning for us.

- Giving up something as a result of giving in to external forces (coercion, enticement, manipulation) is not sacrifice.

- Real sacrifice creates freedom for faith to do its work in developing will, and for commitment, compassion, and love to crystallize within the self.

REFLECTIONS

Following are reflections from those who have worked to apply these concepts of will to their lives as participants in The Leadership Development Forum.

"We cannot see will or describe it objectively. We can however learn to observe and measure its effects in our state, physical functioning, impact on existence, response to adversity, challenge and success . . ."

"When within a group of people; they have faith in one another they build bonds of integrity and gain unassailable strength of character; when they have hope and extend it to one another they illuminate the spirit and open to unlimited energy; when they commit to common work they bring meaning and worth to an effort."

"Rays of hope do not shine on us, they emanate from us and illuminate others."

"The least we can do in life is to take an open and honest shot at building will to become the person we were meant to be. Each of us has innate capacity for this work. Frameworks, stimulating concepts, and guidance by those with experience are necessary . . . but we must do our own work."

"Good leaders clearly and simply layout the work to be done, the worth of it, and an open invitation to become part of the effort . . . then wait to see who shows up."

EVOLVING SELF

Evolving self strives continuously to acquire those aspects of self that are included in our unexplored and undeveloped potential as human beings. Premises about this process include;

- Evolution requires distinctive shifts in essential aspects of behavior; function, being, and will.
- What to shift is a matter for individual unforced decision.
- Decision to shift begins when we come face-to-face with the self that we are and recognize that it is not the self we are meant to become.
- Making the shift is something we can only do for ourselves, although we cannot do it alone. Guides, resources, and powers beyond our own are necessary elements of the process.
- A hierarchy of selves is a valuable guide for our efforts.

MATERIAL SELF

The will becomes conditioned through external forces that ritualistically reward/punish desired/undesired behavior until being goes to sleep and will becomes absorbed in the function at hand. Function occurs in response to direction from the environment or programming deeply imbedded in the self. At extreme, the self is machine-like. Awareness is on full automatic with no experience of inner sensations.

REACTIONAL SELF

Being becomes aware/sensitive that the self is separate from its environment, is a unique entity with a life of its own, and has potential for choice (exercise of will) in performance of functions. This awakening awareness may be initiated when a required function cannot be performed, or when taste for reward or fear of punishment is no longer in control. At extreme, the expression of reactional self will may produce explosive behavior; "I'm mad as hell and I'm not going to take it any more." Reactional self is generally not stable over time.

DIVIDED SELF

The self becomes consciously aware of conflict when response to forces from the environment and response to own core values dictate opposing courses of behavior. The divided self is often an arena of intense, sometimes painful internal struggle when the environment triggers highly conditioned response mechanisms that present strong temptation to betray incompletely tested and integrated core values. From within the self, we *know what is right* and yet have unrelenting forces from the environment that dictate an opposing course.

TRUE SELF

True self is fully awake, aware of behavioral implications of the lower selves and capable of generating behavior most appropriate to the situation at hand. True self maintains a state of calm by *deciding which internal or external stimulus is to be responded to and how.* Doing what is right is weighed in terms of broadest benefit to a greater good while doing no harm in the process. True self reconciles divided self struggle by asking questions like;

- Is this something I can do?
- Is this something I want to do?
- Is this right for me to do?
- Would this lead to a greater good?

In order to shift to a higher self, it is first necessary to manage the present self. A prior condition for managing self is to know the self that is to be managed; what is unknown is unmanageable. Knowing the self is achieved by using processes of self-observing and self-remembering; self-observing to see what is actually going on and self-remembering to compare that to what is intended.

SELF-OBSERVING

Self-observing aims to accurately know behavior not only in terms of its effect and consequence, but also in terms of discovering sources that cause those effects. Managing this process involves;

- Using higher selves to observe those that are lower because a particular self lacks perspective from which to see itself. Impartial and objective observation requires the perspective of divided or true self.

- Effects are seen as result of function, being, and will impact on behavior and the consequence of expressing them.

- Causes are seen in the energy coming from intellectual, emotional, and moving centers.

- Use of appropriate frameworks as a template helps to guide, organize and focus the process.

- Observing involves simply noticing what is going on but is compromised by analysis. The process is essentially effortless and responds to allowing it to take place vs. forcing it. It is necessary to be completely open to whatever is observed vs. working to validate pre-conceived notions.

- Useful knowledge is acquired by identifying patterns of behavior that promote potential for greater good as well as those that tend to be destructive.

SELF-REMEMBERING

The substance of what is to be remembered consists of actively and consciously living our life in accord with a course we have charted that aims to discover and realize a personal destiny. This requires that our actions occur with full realization of who we are, where it is leading us, and what we aim to become. To achieve this experience we must be able to accurately know our behavior and be able to stop, start or modify it at will. The core purpose of self-remembering is acceptance that the essence of being human is to continuously search for purpose in life and to perfect our capability to fulfill this purpose.

CHAPTER XVI

THE WAY FORWARD

WILL TO BECOME . . . TO DO . . . TO BE

Ken Wessel

CHAPTER XVII

THE WAY FORWARD
CHANGE, RENEWAL AND REGENERATION

Change involves; a sustainable shift to a level that includes; commitment to work toward a higher purpose, investment in acquiring skills required to fulfill purpose and natural evolution toward higher states of being.

Renewal includes; return to doing something of value, extending further into the future, replacing what is no longer useful, reconnecting to a promise, and acquiring new energy, enthusiasm or strength.

Regeneration includes; becoming formed as new, moving from a state of decline to a revitalized state, or restoring moral and spiritual values.

PREMISES ABOUT CHANGE

These premises are the foundation for beliefs about change and the source of thinking that has produced frameworks and concepts that present change as a systemic process, based on solid theory with a practical approach to application. Premises are to be tested, validated or modified by those who participate in leadership development seminars.

1. AN ORGANIZATION WILL NOT SURVIVE IN THE ABSENCE OF CHANGE. CHANGE IS FUNDAMENTALLY AN ACT OF CREATING THAT WHICH DOES NOT NOW EXIST, AN ESSENTIAL PROCESS TO SUSTAIN LIFE IN A DYNAMIC UNIVERSE.

    The universe of stakeholders in any organization naturally expect increased value through time and will shift their stake toward most likely source of providing expected value. The organization must be sufficiently engaged with stakeholders to determine what is missing in value needs (even when stakeholder is unaware of specifics) and is in command of change processes that create what does not now exist.

2. PEOPLE AND ORGANIZATIONS TEND TO REGARD PROBLEM SOLVING AND INCREMENTAL IMPROVEMENT AS CHANGE AND THEREFORE OVERLOOK THE REALITY OF CHANGE AS A CRITICAL ELEMENT IN SUSTAINING LIFE.

    Experience of relief at solving chronic and difficult problems create illusion that something has changed even though expenditure of resources to return to standard represents an ultimate drain of organizations vitality. Incremental improvement achieved via redesigns are often cause for celebration that is egoistic in nature and falls short of purposeful intent toward change.

3. LEADERSHIP AND CHANGE ARE INSEPARABLE.

    Effective leaders are oriented to creating desirable futures that integrate core values with vision and realize that change is the only direction to realize their aims. Structural denial of potential to lead change processes will likely cause leaders to withdraw from the field of leadership, to leave the organization and worst of all to channel their leadership capability into non-constructive ventures.

4. LEADERSHIP OF CHANGE MUST COME FROM WITHIN THE SYSTEM BEING CHANGED.

    The untrue adage that "people resist change" ought to be stated as, "people resist being changed." When external influence forces change or when internal authority demands change without involvement of the minds of those affected, so-called "change" is not sustainable because people do not understand it, or accept it, or will undermine it as an act of resistance. By definition, internal leadership involves the minds of those affected in influencing course and impact of what is to be changed. The unique human neo-cortex feels change that evolves, develops and regenerates. "Being changed" stimulates the reactive reptilian brain. (ref: "Evolutions End" J. C. Pearle

5.   TO BE SUCCESSFUL, A LEADER MUST *UNDERSTAND THE NATURE OF CHANGE* AS A CONSEQUENCE OF HIS/HER EXPERIENCE. *KNOWLEDGE* ALONE IS NOT SUFFICIENT.

A great deal of misleading advice calls for management of change based on linear checklists and formula's that are promoted by offering a series of techniques that are to be memorized and applied as a body of "knowledge." Effective leaders come to understand the nature of change by conscious learning from own experience.

6.   CHANGE INVOLVES CREATING INTO A VOID.

Change will not occur when attempting to create something new into what already exists.

7.   MANY CHANGE EFFORTS FAIL OR COME UP SHORT BECAUSE THEIR AGENTS ATTEMPT TO MAKE CHANGE HAPPEN WITHOUT FIRST CREATING POTENTIAL FOR CHANGE TO OCCUR.

Leaders create potential for change by forming a void in own thinking which involves an act of will requiring them to simultaneously hold an accurate, objective picture of current reality and clear view of a more desirable state. Many leaders are overwhelmed by emotional connection to future state, are unable to sustain a void and rush the organization into a change process before potential for change is established. Change as in many physical processes cannot be actualizes unless potential is first established.

8.   THINKING AND COMMUNICATING ABOUT CHANGE IS ENHANCED BY USE OF THINKING FRAMEWORKS THAT INTEGRATE ELEMENTS OF CHANGE INTO A LOGICAL WHOLE.

Use of thinking frameworks stimulate systemic thinking about the whole of a subject, connect elements in a logical pattern and create known, shared reference points for accurate communication of thinking about any specified subject.

9. EFFECTS OF CHANGE REQUIRE SUPERIOR MANAGEMENT; THE PHENOMENON OF CHANGE ITSELF IS HOWEVER, UNMANAGEABLE.

Effective managing requires application of defined managing process to what is known. Leadership involves taking self and/or the organization into unknown territory with sufficient skill to find value in the unknown while minimizing risk.

10. SUSTAINABLE CHANGE REQUIRES THAT A PERSON OR ORGANIZATION FIRST COMMIT TO A HIGHER PURPOSE, ACQUIRE ADVANCED SKILLS NEEDED TO ACHIEVE THAT PURPOSE AND NATURALLY EVOLVE TO HIGHER STATES OF BEHAVIOR.

The first requirement for sustainable change is personal commitment to work for a greater good expressed as a higher purpose. Working for personal gain or self-serving motives is not sustainable in the face of adversity or natural issues that arise. Organizations and individuals often fail to invest in developing skills, resources, materials and assets that are necessary to realize purpose and as a result create frustration due to unfulfilled aims. A combination of higher purpose and capability to fulfill it, naturally produces elevated states in terms of self-confidence, partnering, optimism, desire to serve others, stewardship etc.

11. SUSTAINABLE CHANGE IS GROUNDED IN AN OBJECTIVELY ACCURATE GRASP OF REALITY.

Firm and energizing ground as source for initiating change requires an accurate and truthful grasp of reality, including healthy dissatisfaction with current state. Emotional rejection of current state of affairs often initiates reckless, unthinking, leaderless venturing into the unknown. An accurate appraisal of current state is a valuable source of skills and resources that support the change process and develop natural ownership of the process and what is to be created.

LEADERSHIP: RENEWAL AND REGENERATION

The aim of this paper is to provide those who have will to lead, guidance in how to recognize and take advantage of everyday opportunity to express their leadership.

All who have some level of will to lead have experienced desire, impulse or urge to take on a leadership role but have been uncertain about the nature of need for leadership and opportunity for them to provide it. Therefore as they struggle with decision to step forward the window of opportunity may close and need for leadership remains unsatisfied.

Not surprisingly, opportunity for leadership is a function of an unsatisfied need for leadership. And as we have learned, leadership and change are inseparable, therefore need and/or opportunity for change in a situation is a clear call for leadership.

Evidence of need for change and development can be seen as:
- A loss or decline of purpose to a degree that people no longer find focus, meaning, or motivation from their work

- Absence or dramatic decline of emotional, mental, and/or physical energy invested in work

- Levels of capability and competence inadequate to produce acceptable performance.

Evidence of these conditions is therefore a call for leadership to influence a shift to distinctively higher levels of purpose, state and function. Experience tells us that processes of managing and supervising are not sufficient to energize these shifts.

Need and opportunity for change and development can be found in virtually any everyday situation, where for example;

- People are frustrated by inability to solve a chronic problem "once and for all" and find like Sisyphus, "they never get the stone to top of the hill."

- People intuitively recognize opportunity to improve something or themselves, but cannot conceive how to go about doing it

- Forces in their environment demand change as means for survival

- Forces within the organization demand change as means for personal and organization growth and development
  When need for leadership is recognized, the next step is to apply leaders will to existing issues, for example when:

- People cannot visualize the desired end-state their work will produce for themselves and others and they lack inner drive to sustain an effort. Therefore, a leader must stimulate a motivating vision.

- Core values of individuals are not involved in their work, or their values are in conflict with the way in which they are working. Therefore, a leader must stimulate awareness of personal core values and support people in living by them.

- People lack influence in change process and are fearful of adverse effect it might have. Therefore, a leader must involve people in defining a path of change that aims to fulfill their vision and in managing events that affect them.

- People become accustomed to mediocrity as the norm and produce results "not to be proud of" and that do not merit recognition from others. Therefore, a leader must challenge them to establish high ideals as benchmarks for working toward perfection.

It is essential that leaders direct the application of will to processes that change the nature of work and the way work is done such that greater value is produced for the benefit of themselves and their stakeholders.

CHAPTER XVII

THE WAY FORWARD

CHANGE, RENEWAL AND REGENERATION

Ken Wessel

CHAPTER XVIII

THE WAY FORWARD

IT CAN BE DONE BECAUSE IT IS BEING DONE

A DEVELOPMENTAL JOURNEY

A <u>journey</u> is not a trip or a commute. Properly understood, a journey is a worthwhile, remarkable, and exciting undertaking that proceeds into the unknown, finds value in discovery, and faces up to the risks involved.

<u>Development</u> is a special form of change that is initiated from what is (present state) and aims to create new and higher order states through;

- Pursuit of higher purposes
- Advancing the character and integrity of culture
- Step change in essential skill and capability to do work

These characteristics apply to personal and organization development.

Each developmental journey is unique and at the same time follows known and predictable patterns. Unknown and unexpected opportunities and hazards present themselves along the way, although a wise leader with the help of an experienced guide, will find advantage in opportunity as well as hazard.

Making a journey involves four stages, initiating, organizing, launching and evolving. Stages proceed in a natural sequence although they are iterative and overlap.

<u>Initiation</u>

- Development can only occur in a climate of healthy dissatisfaction with the current state.

- Activating a shift from current organization state requires critical mass of personal values from a nucleus of those who will lead the journey.

- Journey is focused by leader's vision of a better, future state for themselves and others in which their values are expressed.

- Potential for movement is energized by missions that stimulate values of those who would join the journey and invite them to work for its success.

Planning Teams of capable leaders are formed to initiate the journey.

Organization

Five fully integrated roles are essential for success in the journey. Each of these roles is focused on journey's purpose (consistent with leader's vision) and invested in its mission.

- Role of leading challenges the organization to draw on their unique capabilities and focus them on objectives that simultaneously achieve business advantage and a more highly developed organization. No person or organization ought to embark on a journey or expect to develop, in the absence of effective leading. Planning Teams have played this role in initiating many successful journeys.

- Role of managing uses principles as guides to a high road of thinking, action, and behavior in the organizations journey. Managing is ideally applied to things but must also be appropriately applied to people (in the role of supervising) when they lack capability to self-manage to those principles. This role is normally filled by Leadership Teams which have challenged individual members to proactively lead or supervise their own organization as appropriate. As objectives become more demanding, managing excellence becomes more critical.

- Role of working obligates *all* organization members to step up to roles and perform functions that make measurable contributions to success of their unit, site, and business. *Each* person has accountability to produce explicitly stated results that achieve current standards, work for success of business/site/unit objectives, continuously improve self, and uphold principles of the organization. Engaging *every* member of the organization at this level continues to be a significant challenge. It seems clear that proactively choosing to lead/supervise at all levels is the key to engaging the *entire organization* as full time workers for the journey.

- Role of <u>coaching</u> builds into the organization and its members those functional and behavioral skills that are required to do their work and perform their roles at increasingly higher levels of capability. Coaching is done in the context of "real work" by individuals who are credible in terms of their personal experience, commitment to the journey, and desire for success of their pupils. Coaching and the related role of mentoring aim to develop the individual as a part of increasing their functional capability. Examples of coaching successful journeys include; role redesign, networking safety, developing functional teams, leading edge technology programs, etc. Essential nature of effective coaching becomes clear when people commit to roles that are beyond present capability and demand training and development required to close the gap.

- Role of <u>guiding</u> includes the presence and active involvement of someone who has experience in similar journeys. This experience makes it possible to see the journey as a whole, including the relationship of day to day events to its intended destination and to see opportunities and hazards that are invisible to the less experienced. Guiding brings an external perspective and source of support for all other roles.

<u>Launching</u>

Launching involves activating essential roles, infusing them with initiating force and energy and connecting them such that they are able to pull together in pursuit of shared goals. Part of the journey at this stage was to develop and agree on a number of critical factors that could individually determine success or failure in the journey. These included;

- The business must increase its competitive position and strength.

- Sites must make distinctive measurable strides toward operational excellence.

- Primary external customer connections must follow the material flow vs. chain of command or functional silos.

- Each person and unit needs to measure their contribution in terms that support site and business goals. Status must be routinely audited, with feedback and course correction as needed.

- A core methodology for organization design and development needs to be selected, invested in and practiced throughout.

- Work on objectives and projects follow a clearly laid out, comprehensive plan of attack. Everyday work follows agreed to, written procedures and aims to achieve specifically stated performance and behavioral standards.

- Every organization member has made a conscious choice to step into a role that makes an essential contribution. Taking a position on the sidelines or in the bleachers is unacceptable.

- Boundary interface with headquarters needs to be managed such that positive energy flows both ways and attention is diverted from guarding boundaries to cooperation across the interface.

Evolution

The conduct of a successful journey evolves along the way as a consequence of activities and events that are initiated, experience gained, impact of unforeseen influences, increased access to useful resources and shifts in thinking of leaders. For many organizations these include;

- Self-designed and self-led leadership team meetings.

- Extension of goals, objectives, key measures, and useful techniques from leadership teams into the organization through networks, task teams and chain of command.

- Involvement of leadership team members and others in strategic planning process focused on business results supported by operational excellence.

- Increased direct involvement of local personnel at headquarters in leadership team events and activities.

- Islands of distinctive development are scattered throughout, although a broad scale wave of change is yet to come.

- Changing membership of the management team such that current members are inclined toward teamwork, are credible in their own organizations and have a leadership bent.

- Struggle with issues that lead to an unsatisfactory level of execution. These include unclear roles, lack of confidence in being proactive as leader/supervisor, grip of "old culture/ environment", absence of well-designed and practiced audit/ feedback/course correcting process.

- Recognition that a complex and challenging journey is subject to the law of entropy and must from time to time re-new and rededicate itself.

Degree to which these factors are in place, understood, and are influential has been spotty in many organizations and should be a high priority subject for attention and upgrade.

Of all the factors that define what a journey is and whether it is likely to succeed, none is more critical than personal core values of its leaders. Without a leader there is no journey, nor is there development and without conscious dedication to uphold own core values, there is insufficient will to persevere as a leader. It is necessary to differentiate core values from other forms and depths of value. For example a common functional value is to support safety and environmental programs. At greater depth is value that no one or the planet gets hurt. And at the core of personal values is commitment to work for the physical and psychological well being of others. Regeneration of the journey must include discovery and sharing of core values among its leaders.

I leave it to you the reader to use the concepts of "A Developmental Journey" as a means to evaluate organizations where you have or wish to have a stakeholder relationship and others that you are knowledgeable about. Without aiming to dot I's and cross T's, place organizations in the following framework and reflecting on basis for your choices will stimulate your experience and add to understanding of what leading a developmental journey is about.

JOURNEY

STUCK	UNDERWAY
NONE-COST CUTTING	
DEVELOPMENT INVESTMENT	
FUTURE ORIENTED	

INCREASING DEPTH AND BREADTH OF SKILL

The intent of this subject is to present elements involved in the activity of progressing to increasingly higher levels of skill as measured by depth of capability, in such a way as to stimulate and organize thinking about the design of structures, systems and processes that enable orderly development of people and predictable increases in their contribution and as basis to reflect on progress/lack of progress in organizations with which you are familiar.

As such, concepts of depth as presented apply to any defined field of endeavor (medicine, managing manufacturing operations, accounting, music) although the breadth dimension must be described in terms of functions that are characteristic of a specified field. Fields may be described broadly (music could include; composing, conducting, performing, teaching, arranging) or narrowly (teaching music could include; class preparation, instruments, voice, dance, directing musical productions.)

The challenge to individuals and their organizations is to design a structure that includes breadth and depth dimensions relevant to organization purposes that guide role definition and performance to include specified aspects of breadth and depth. Roles must distinctively different from and additive to other roles, and within the capacity of organization members to acquire and perform well.

When structure is defined the next challenge is to design systems of progression that feature development along a predetermined (although flexible) path where a person builds from base up in terms of depth and in a logical sequence of learning to successfully practice additional functions. Levels of work and elements of activity in structuring each level are base up phenomena with higher levels building on lower levels and lower levels retaining their intrinsic value.

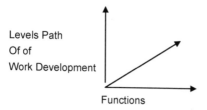

Levels Path
Of of
Work Development

Functions

Levels of work refers to depth and functions to breadth. Path of development must note that each dimension can be taken to extreme; "knowing everything about nothing" or "knowing nothing about everything." This paper will examine the structuring of depth in terms of levels of work, building from a specific framework.

Empowerment Of Achievement

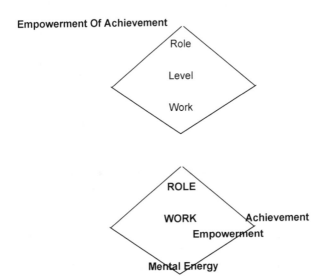

EMPOWERMENT is the grounding element in the activity of progressing to higher levels of work. It has to do with increasing mastery of one's inner powers such that they become a firm foundation from which to progress and are a reliable source of energy for the process.

ACHIEVEMENT refers to the distinctive goal of each level of work with the expectation that value of contribution and terms of success increase with each level. It is presented as it relates to business pursuits.

ROLE is defined using the ancient Guild system as analogy, to depict the direction of personal growth and development.

MENTAL ENERGY describes thought energy in qualitative terms and is the instrument that a person must learn to use as primary means for progressing in depth of skill.

The core structure is presented as five levels of work; stabilize, operate, maintain, improve, and regenerate. The distinctive quality of each will be described along with each of the four elements of developmental activity required to progress to a specified level. It is understood that the connection between each element of the framework is significant as well as the meaning of the element itself.

STABILIZING WORK

This is work required to hold conditions at a level above irreparable damage and/or to prevent irreversible undesirable effects.

Empowerment: A person demonstrates they are a **good householder**, are able to take care of personal affairs such that they are not a burden to others and do not initiate upset in their environment.

Achievement: Business is able to buy time and create space needed to block downside effects while acting to initiate movement to higher levels.

Role: Joining a particular Guild requires that a person step forward as a **candidate** and submit themselves to selection standards of the particular field or profession. For example a person must demonstrate the traits of a good householder (no tramps, fools, or thieves) and potential to progress to higher levels of work.

Mental energy: **Automatic** thought energy perceives and builds a habit of doing those mundane tasks well that are necessary to sustain life. **Vital** energy kicks in and issues a wakeup call when the system is at risk or facing a threat. (Note that when automatic energy is not available, threat response tends to be driven by emotional and/or physical energy that often makes the crisis more acute.)

OPERATING WORK

Work required to consistently achieve current standards in the presence of ordinary variances.

Empowerment: A person demonstrates their power of **self-discipline** in following specified procedures, abiding by rules and guidelines, and working to standards. They demonstrate their power of self-denial when doing the right thing involves performing tasks found to be unpleasant or in letting go of that which gives them pleasure but fails to add value.

Achievement: Business is able to retain its stakeholder base in static situations, but is at high risk of losing their support in a dynamic environment of rising stakeholder needs and expectations and aggressive competitive challenge.

Role: It is as **apprentice** that a person demonstrates their capability to submit to the teachings, procedures, rules, standards and guidelines that define the field they are entering. Aptitude for and attraction to the nature of functions they take on are fundamental requirements of the role. Caring for tools, materials, workplace and welfare of others is fundamental, as is respect for standards of self-conduct.

Mental energy: It is **sensitive** mental energy that perceives a variance from standard and **automatic** energy that responds through deliberately acquired work habits. It is the coupling of these energies that enables keeping a process more or less on standard. It should be noted that automatic does not mean thoughtless, but rather disciplined programming of actions. Presence of sensitive energy insures that corrective action has the desired effect and if not will call for further adjustment that may involve higher levels of work.

ADVANCING WORK

Work that draws on experience as a source of discovering methods for doing work that moves toward perfection or the ideal. This leads to advanced procedures, higher standards and capability to achieve them in a wide range of circumstances.

Empowerment: Command of inner powers of **self-initiative** and **self-direction** is essential to the task of advancing work performance toward the ideal. By contrast, waiting for others to tell us what to do or point the way, is certain to reinforce the status quo, especially if things are generally OK.

Achievement: Business is able to maintain pace with growing customer needs and most competitors in ordinary circumstances.

Role: **Journeyman** has demonstrated desire and capability to move beyond initial sources of teaching and learning in order to meet the challenges of perfecting skills in the "real world" of application. Learning from own experience and taking initiative to invest that learning in increasing the value from one's work is the commonly accepted sign of an empowered person. What is often overlooked in this view is the requirement that exercise of self-initiative be grounded in self-discipline as evidenced by serving a successful apprenticeship, subject to judgment by a **Master** that the time is right.

<u>Mental Energy:</u> **Conscious** mental energy enables an objective view of the work itself, the way work is done, products of work, and oneself doing the work as a dynamic and realistic whole. Exercise of this energy blended with **sensitive** energy, enables shifts in procedures and standards that lead to higher value products and are yet in tune with experience and what is acceptable in the work environment.

IMPROVING WORK

Work required to design/redesign current products, technology, and organizations and to manage implementation projects, such that current, common variances are no longer possible and concepts of perfection are redefined.

<u>Empowerment:</u> The power of **self-accountability** is essential to successful performance of improving level work because it enables a person to accept the consequence of own actions and behavior:
Without blaming (self or others), justifying or rationalizing the effect of improvement efforts that fail to "work out right." These behaviors conspire to shut down learning from experience and discourage future improvement efforts.

- Without seeking or expectation of a special reward when things work out well or better than anticipated. Promise of reward including recognition, can incline a person often in subtle ways, to work for the reward at the expense of "working for the work or working for the result." By definition, whomever controls the reward has a measure of control over a person who is working with expectation of being rewarded, given particular outcomes. Reward systems thinking is rampant in present organizations and is a primary source of disempowerment.

- <u>Achievement:</u> Business is able to create a distinctive competitive edge and sustain it in a wide variety of business situations.

<u>Role:</u> **Craftsman** has demonstrated commitment to work to standards of excellence that represent a personal challenge to existing skill and an ongoing demand for increasing it. These standards are always beyond what are necessary to "get by." Capability to perform at this level is more self-taught than learned from others, and higher order tools and techniques are created out of personal experience vs. taken "off the shelf," or copied from others. True **Craftsmen** are open to praise and criticism from others, but ultimately their own judgment prevails.

<u>Mental Energy:</u> **Creative** mental energy enables a person to see what does not exist, and to hold that thought while **consciously** pursuing a course of bringing it into existence.

REGENERATING WORK

Work required to bring new generations of product, technology, or organization into existence. It is characterized by step change between what is and what is to become.

<u>Empowerment:</u> The powers of self-initiative, self-discipline, and self-accountability have come together in a fully integrated and crystallized form such that a person is not susceptible to disruptive external or internal influence. A **true self** is in command.

<u>Achievement:</u> Business has internalized change and development as essential elements of what it is and has become a leading force for change and evolution of the industry.

<u>Role:</u> **Masters** take on the role of stewards for the future of the guild, craft, or profession. In this role they constantly seek to expand dimensions of skill, product values, reputation, and integrity of the guild. They achieve this by evolution of technique, product, organization and people. Masters have the last word on who enters and progresses in the craft and on what techniques and products represent the working of the craft.

<u>Mental Energy:</u> **Unitive** mental energy enables perceptive visioning of a future where elements that are separate, isolated, and non-existent in the present come together in new, different, useful and ultimately natural forms. The effect of this energy is to raise new possibilities into which voids

can be formed by use of **creative** energy such that something different and better can be brought into existence.

ORGANIZATIONAL USE OF THIS MATERIAL

Organizations that have successfully incorporated these concepts have previously committed to a course of organization redesign and development and have enabled that course with capable leadership and necessary resources. They will be operating from a motivating vision of what they aim to become, a philosophy that states their commitment to action, and an objectively clear view of the business they are in and the value adding work required for success. They will have internalized throughout the organization principles that guide the thinking and actions or all members. Following are principles they tend to use to guide progression:

- Successful demonstration of performance and contribution in roles base on a specified level of work is a condition for moving to a higher level.
- A person is expected to maintain capability to perform satisfactorily at any level for which they have been judged to be qualified.
- Steady progress through levels including Advancing Level is a condition of employment.
- The organization supports progression by providing capable systems of selection, orientation, training, performance appraisal and improvement, and career planning.

PERSONAL USE OF THIS MATERIAL

An individual may gain useful knowledge by approaching the material in this way:

1. Acquire a sense of the whole of it by scanning
2. Read more carefully taking note of subjects, phrases, or concepts that have definite appeal or stimulate special energy.
3. Set it aside and come back to it with intent to make specific connections to elements of own experience and/or subjects of present interest and activity.
4. Use this material to design a process to assess own career path and career progression systems in your organizations and to get a feel for what is actually being done in current times.

5.   Look for a practical way to apply these concepts to enhance own career progression and as basis for designing a systemic approach to increasing depth, breadth and extension of skill in your organizations.

Gaining a useful understanding of this material requires work with others who are like-minded with guidance by someone who has direct experience with these concepts in a variety of circumstances.

1.   The following references may be useful for further study:
2.   For levels of mental energy; "Energies" by John G. Bennett
3.   For background frameworks; "Elementary Systematics" by John G. Bennett
4.   For Guild System; "The Way of the Craftsman" by Macnulty
5.   For personal empowerment; "Empowerment; Desired State for Any Person" by KH Wessel

CHAPTER XVIII

THE WAY FORWARD

IT CAN BE DONE BECAUSE IT IS BEING DONE